CW00920941

A Guide to Castles in Radnorshire

Monuments in the Landscape

Volume III

A Guide to Castles in Radnorshire

by
Paul Martin Remfry

Logaston Press

LOGASTON PRESS
Little Logaston Woonton Almeley
Herefordshire HR3 6QH

First published by Logaston Press 1996
Copyright © Paul Remfry 1996

All rights reserved. No part of this publication
may be reproduced, stored in a retrieval system,
or transmitted, in any form or by any means,
electronic, mechanical, photocopying, recording
or otherwise, without the prior permission,
in writing of the publisher.

ISBN 1 873827 54 7

Set in Times 11/13 pt by Logaston Press
and printed in Great Britain by The Cromwell Press, Melksham

Please Note

The following points must be observed when visiting sites:

1. Always follow the Countryside Code.

2. On all sites, extreme care should be taken.

3. Any artefacts found within the county should be reported to the County Archaeological Officer or at any local museum.

4. Under no circumstances should visitors dig around or on any site. Any damage could result in prosecution.

5. It is an offence under the 1979 Ancient Monuments and Archaeological Areas Act to use metal detectors on or near scheduled ancient monuments. In addition, simple 'treasure hunting' near ancient monuments can well damage evidence to such an extent that archaeologists are unable to interpret it fully in the future.

Contents

Acknowledgments

I would like to thank all those who, over the years, have aided in the design, writing, checking and publication of this book. Especially I would like to thank all those archaeological and historical friends and acquaintances who have toiled in the libraries and in the field, visiting and recording literary references and visiting all the castles that appear here within. I have enjoyed many happy hours with such a variety of companions in the invigorating search for an understanding of the military actions of our distant forebears. I would particularly wish to thank Brian Byron for drawing the maps and plans, Betty Lloyd of Painscastle for permission to use the aerial photograph of Painscastle, whilst copyright for that of Cymaron lies with Clwyd-Powys Archaeological Trust (Photograph number 86-MB-1184).

Paul Martin Remfry,
Malvern, July 1996

Bibliography

Most of the information contained in this book is taken from the series of monographs written by Paul Remfry on castles. A full bibliography of all the works used for historical references are found there. Information on these works and the new 'Fighting Castles' series is available from SCS Publishing, 31 Richmond Road, Malvern Link, Worcs. WR14 1NE. A note on the general sources is, however, given in the Introduction.

Introduction

The old county of Radnorshire is, relatively speaking, not an ancient land unit. It was formed in 1536 when Henry VIII abolished the Marcher Lordships of Wales and created counties in their wake. In 1974 the 471 square mile shire that Henry had ordered to be created was itself swept away, being engulfed into the larger county of Powys. Any historical justification for this name being applied to Radnorshire is highly questionable, although the economics of the union is another matter.

Castles were built in this district before Radnorshire, as such, was formed. During the early Middle Ages the shire consisted of the remnants of several Welsh land units called cantrefs and their sub-divisions known as commotes. These lands, after 1066, had been intermittently conquered by the new Norman lords of the Welsh Marches. Welsh re-conquests had added to the political confusion and fragmentation of the area. As a consequence of this it is now difficult to reconstruct the actual boundaries of these older land units. By 1200, most of these cantrefs and commotes had been submerged under new Marcher lordships. Some like Clun, Radnor and Painscastle had Norman names, others like Maelienydd and Elfael kept their older Welsh forms. All suffered frequent disruptions in the incessant fighting that gripped the area between 1093 and 1282.

Geographically and historically, by the twelfth century Radnorshire consisted of several constituent parts, namely the cantrefs of Maelienydd (less the commote of Ceri), Elfael (which included Radnor, known to the later Welsh as Llythyfnwg) and the commotes of Gwrtheyrnion, and Elenydd or Cwmwd Deuddwr. All

1

these regions consisted of highland moor, generally with underlying sandstones, such as at Radnor Forest, Clun Forest, and the Cambrian Mountains; and lowland fertile areas, generally along the line of the river valleys of the Wye and Eithon. Most of the region exceeds 600 feet above sea level, and just over half of it is above 1,000 feet. The sandstone Plynlimon range occupies the western-most area of the county and is the highest point of the central moor-lands of Wales, which, consisting primarily of boulder clay, is mostly a cold, waterlogged bog of wet sub-soils. Cutting through the entire region in deep valleys are the main rivers, the Wye and Teme flowing south-east, the Lugg and Arrow flowing east from Radnor Forest, and the Eithon flowing from north to south into the Wye. These valleys form the low lying pastures on which modern-day agriculture is still based, consisting as they do of large quantities of recent alluvium which accounts for much of the fertility. Glacial drift or debris, which together with alluvium forms the main building material for mottes, is widespread throughout the region and probably accounts for the predominance of mottes over stone-built castle ringworks.

The climate of Radnorshire is generally cool, with damp summers and mild wet winters. However the relief creates surprising contrasts. The fertile lower Wye valley can be some 6°F warmer than the mountainous Radnor Forest, whilst the rainfall in the western mountains averages 80 inches per annum against only 35 inches in the eastern valleys. This east-west contrast is again apparent as the western part of the region consists of poor acid soils with peat developing on the wet, badly drained moors and hilltops, whilst the lower lying eastern alluvium soils become more fertile the nearer they are towards the Old Red Sandstone of the Herefordshire plains. The original deciduous forests of Leland's day and earlier have largely disappeared before the advance of modern agriculture in the lower lying valleys. On the slopes above the valleys the hills are covered with rough pastures which grade upwards into heather coated moors. Below 1,000 feet, the land is now largely enclosed in fields of grass, generally of *Agrostis* with rushes on the fields which are poorly drained. Only in the eastern lowlands and in the low lying Llandrindod and Llanelwedd areas is there the better *Agrostis-rye* grass pasture. It is an area well-suited

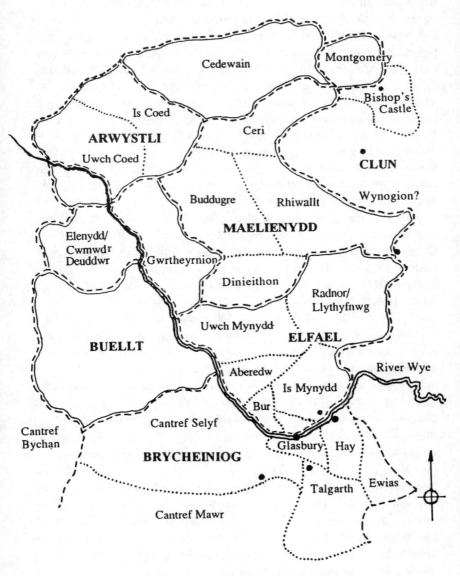

**Cantrefs and Commotes
Rhwng Gwy a Hafren**

to the breeding of sheep and store cattle. Even today the area is one of the most thinly populated in England and Wales.

Leland's account of Maelienydd some four hundred years after the days of Cadwallon ap Madog, is worth noting. According to him part of 'Melenith' was still well wooded, but the rest was 'scant'. In certain areas there was plenty of corn and of course 'great plenty of grass'. There was also a good breed of horse called Herdell in the mountains and all manner of cattle. No more than fifty years later Radnor Forest was described as 2,000 acres of waste heath, wild, foggy, marsh ground, and only 8 acres of low shrubs and thorn bushes. It would therefore appear that other than the deforestation and better agricultural methods, Radnorshire has not changed greatly over the past millennium.

The geology of the region also determined the uneven distribution of castles within it, as few castles existed in the more forbidding mountains and wastes of the west, where the population was also less dense. The distribution of castles in Radnorshire appears to have been: 1 in Elenydd, 27 in Elfael (including 11 in Radnor/Llythyfnwg), 2 in Gwrtheyrnion and 15 in Maelienydd making a total of 45 sites. Of these, the following 21 have at least one mention as being a castle in historical sources between 1066 and 1536: 1 in Elenydd, 8 in Elfael (including 1 in Radnor/Llythyfnwg), 1 in Gwrtheyrnion and 11 in Maelienydd.

The little or lack of mention of so many castles may at first seem daunting to the historian, but in the case of the chief castles of the old Welsh commotes there is a greater degree of historical knowledge. Thus we find the story of the 'lordship castles' (as one might term them) fairly well documented. The history of the major castles like Radnor, Cymaron, Cefnllys, Painscastle, Colwyn, Boughrood and the like is fairly clear. That castles fell and were retaken without record is certain, but when they were of strategic importance like the chief castle of a commote or lordship, they were likely to find mention somewhere in contemporary record. This is especially true from the mid-twelfth century onwards, when such records begin to proliferate.

The sources

The history of all the cantrefs and commotes which composed the land of Radnorshire in the main castle building age, 1070 to 1285, is generally scant. The bulk of the documentary evidence comes from royal records and monastic chronicles. There are few non-royal transactions or documents of use. Most of these are land grants to Cadwallon ap Madog's abbey of Cwmhir. Thankfully the Welsh Chronicles sketch in barest outline some of the recorded history of these provinces.

Additional to these, and extremely useful for the Middle Marches of Wales, is the fourteenth century Mortimer Genealogy. The original manuscript is now in the Chicago University Library. It is not a complete text, as printed by Dugdale, but a short history of the foundation of Wigmore Abbey and a Mortimer genealogy, with many interpolations where space permits, taken out of context from the rest of the work. Thus is the curious rambling repetitive style of Dugdale's 'History' explained. The original manuscript commences with a detailed Anglo-Norman account of the foundation of Wigmore Abbey. It is written in a fourteenth century court hand that does not appear elsewhere in the manuscript and would appear to have been written soon after the death of Isabella Mortimer on 31 May, 1252, as it mentions her in the past tense. It would also appear to suggest that the author had seen Oliver Merlymond (d.c.1150) both alive and dead. Obviously the time span of this opening foundation history would indicate, as well as the fourteenth century court hand, that this is some form of composite text, possibly put into its present form some time after the 1350s. Despite this the content of the foundation text appears to be original. There is no material in it that is demonstrably false, and much that is demonstrably true. Therefore the reliability of the uncorroborated statements in this chronicle should be regarded more favourably than the late date of the manuscript might suggest.

The opening account of the foundation of Wigmore Abbey is followed by various minor works and then the main Mortimer genealogy. This genealogy is reproduced word for word by Dugdale, but without reference to the various hands that wrote it, or the fact that this part of the work is divided into various independent boxed sections. These texts, the bulk of the manuscript, probably date to the very end of the fourteenth century, as they finish with Roger, the fourth earl of March, who died in 1398. However, in the genealogy itself there are several erroneous interpolations of a probably only slightly later hand, which have earned Dugdale's account an unfair low standing for reliability. Events related in the text bear a strong resemblance to a Latin copy of a Welsh Chronicle and suggests that the compilor may have been using source material now no longer available to us. It is unfortunate that both these 'Mortimer histories' only bring the political problems and objectives of the Mortimers into view when they become involved with the affairs of the abbey. They therefore offer a far from complete account of the lives of the lords of Wigmore themselves.

Of great help in distinguishing the various Welsh characters who regularly appear in various other documents, are the later genealogies in the British Museum and the National Library of Wales. Most of these genealogical sources have been compiled by P.C. Bartrum, but as he himself notes, these mainly fifteenth century works cannot be regarded by any means as one hundred per cent accurate. Giraldus Cambrensis is a source of the greatest importance when supplying materials of specific detail on the affairs of Radnorshire which would otherwise have stood little chance of having been preserved. Ordericus Vitalis is also of great value for the earliest periods of the Norman Conquest, but it must be remembered that Orderic was writing from Normandy about his homeland around Shrewsbury, which he had left when young. Some caution must also be shown in making use of the various monastic chronicles from which much information is drawn, as most commence as compilations, copies, or worse. The best of these concerning the Middle March is undoubtedly the so-called chronicle of Benedict of Peterborough, which was compiled roughly contemporaneously with the events it describes, and was apparently copied in part by Roger of Hoveden. The Pipe Rolls and later, the Close, Patent and Charter Rolls, are less liable to the distortions of the chroniclers, and play a major role in the narrative, being used extensively from the mid-twelfth century onwards. Information additional to these chronicles can be drawn from the poetry of the era, but this must be recognized as an extremely hazardous source.

This leaves just one other source to be drawn upon, the archaeological evidence. In Radnorshire this manifests itself, as elsewhere, pre-eminently in the advance of the castle. However, great caution must be used when attempting to utilize this evidence, for whilst castle designs varied over the years, individual sites were unsystematically altered as new military innovations occurred. Increasingly, excavation has proved that even apparently simple sites often have more than one phase of building, and it is next to impossible to relate these phases to the terse entries of castle building and destruction in various documents concerning the Welsh March. So, added to the unreliable structural remnants of these fortresses, are the continual problems of accurate dating and even of assessing what the present remains actually once were. Yet in Radnorshire the castles appear to have settled into a fairly standard pattern, although there is still a wide range for variation and discrepancy.

Terminology
One of the first problems is the definition of terminology. In this book the following terms are used: 'Motte' refers to a conical mound, either artificial or a scarped natural outcrop, that was raised with the probable intention of supporting a tower or a small keep of some description, but not a fortified inner ward. Examples of such mottes may be found in Radnorshire at Aberedw, Burfa, Cae Maerdy, Penarth, Crug Eryr, Cymaron, Dolbedwin, Evenjobb, Fforest, Glan Edw, Kinnerton, Knighton, Llandeilo Graben, Norton, Painscastle, Stanage, Tomen and Womaston. 'Mound' refers to a mound, artificial or natural, that has been used primarily as the castle proper, or inner ward, the defences of which would have obviously consisted of more than a single tower. Examples include the inner ward at New Radnor and Colwyn.

The descriptions of other types of inner defences also pose problems. 'Ringwork' is used to mean a circular or ellipsoid ditch and rampart, where there appears to have been no attempt to raise the level of the interior artificially. Examples of this type appear at Castell Nimble, Twyn y Garth and maybe Cwm y Saeson if this is a castle. A 'raised ringwork' would therefore be defined as a ringwork whose interior has been obviously artificially raised as at Presteign and possibly Tinboeth, though it is to be noted that this apparent artificial raising of the interior has often been found on excavation to be the result of drift and silting after the abandonment of the site. A 'ditched enclosure' is similar to a ringwork, but has no rampart. Examples of such ditched enclosures are few, but one would appear to have existed next to the church at Old Radnor. Such sites are generally, and possibly erroneously, regarded as fourteenth century or later.

Then we have the problem of masonry remains, which in some ways are even trickier than earthworks. First of all it has to be said that many so called earthwork castles did in fact at some point in their lives contain masonry. In Radnorshire it can be seen that many previously unrecognised stone castles have been uncovered by systematic field work and detailed examinations. Excavation at similar sites has confirmed the likelihood of these castles being stone structures. At Bryn Amlwg in Clun Lordship what was thought to have been a ringwork was found on excavation to have been a powerful masonry castle, with towers and an advanced gatehouse. Other comparisons in Wales and the March, and no doubt beyond, show that such mal-classifications are not uncommon.

The dating of such masonry structures is a hazardous task, but wherever possible this is attempted and comparable structures of known date are mentioned. However, it is to be remembered that comparable structures need not be contemporary, and historical reference to building at a site is a far better, though still inaccurate, guide to age.

The castles

In order to place the castles of Radnorshire in context it is necessary to have a brief review of what is known of the evolution of the castle. There are no certain stone structures of pre-Conquest (1066) date in Great Britain. (The keep at Richard's Castle in adjoining Herefordshire is believed to have been built in stone before the Conquest, but there is no definite evidence.) In comparison in Anjou and Touraine they abound, viz. the hall of Langeais and the keep of Montbazon, 991-4, the keep of Montrichard built by 1005, and the keeps of Loches and Loudun which date to before 1028. There are also castles in Normandy that appear to be early works, viz. Doué-la-Fontaine, Ivry la Bataille, Plessis, Brion and Freteval all of which appear to have had stone components before 1047. However, of all the early castles very few, if any, appear to be motte and bailey structures. Promontory ringworks, some probably raised, with or without baileys, being far more common, e.g. at Ivry la Bataille, Tillieres, Falaise and Domfront. Despite these Continental and English variations, Radnorshire seems to have arrived at a relatively standard castle building pattern in so far as the first castle built in a region was that at the centre of a new lordship, or old commote. This major fortress was then surrounded by smaller fortresses, built by the knights who held their lands from, and owed service at, the major castle.

The physical positioning of castles in the landscape was always of crucial importance. There must have been a multitude of reasons for founding a castle in its chosen position; changes of site—rarely more than once—did occur. Royal castles were generally built as administrative centres or to overawe a settlement. Major barons built their principal fortresses both for comfort and show. Others were merely constructed for strategic purposes, guarding exposed vills and as outposts for the adventurers on those dangerous frontiers. Perhaps we can also look to royal authority for castle siting. In Normandy the customs of the Duchy (1091), forbade the erection of castles without licence, and from the Welsh angle, most importantly, forbade their construction on rocks or islands, presumably because of their great natural strength. Perhaps here is one reason for the early Norman castles of Wales and the March generally being low lying, unlike many of those early castles of Normandy mentioned above. In the whole of Wales the only certain early Norman sites deliberately occupying high ground are Degannwy (Gwynedd), Tomen y Mur (Gwynedd) which occupies a flat platform overlooked by a hill, Dinas Powys (Glamorgan) and Dinas (Lordship of Brecon), together with the castles tentatively assigned to the Welsh.

From the first, some of the castles in Wales must have been constructed in stone, Chepstow, probably Monmouth and apparently Degannwy being the first. Even though direct evidence of castle dating is hard to come by, that is not to say that it does not exist. White Castle in Monmouthshire offers fairly firm dating evidence, and shows the changing style of fortification throughout

9

the early Middle Ages. It started life as a raised ringwork (or possibly a ditched enclosure), then received a square stone keep before 1186 (foundations remain to the south) when it is mentioned, and finally a polygonal curtain wall, probably in 1188, followed by numerous additions in the thirteenth century. Yet some important Marcher castles were never fortified in stone. Hen Domen, Montgomery, despite being in a state of fortification as late as the end of the thirteenth century was always an earth and timber castle. This immediately throws doubts on the traditional view of the Welsh March. Instead of flimsily built wooden structures protecting isolated settlements we have major earth, wood and stone fortifications which must have been invulnerable to all but the most determined of native attacks. In the plain of Radnor alone we seem to have nine castle sites of which five were certainly stone, and most likely date to the twelfth century or earlier. The removal of the garrisons from these sites must have been next to impossible for the local Welsh; castles only falling to them due to either a surprise attack, treachery, or, as will be seen, most commonly by the collapse of Norman will to hold down a district. This obviously fits in well with the Welsh resurgences only occurring at times of Norman upheaval in other areas of what was to become the Angevin empire.

Later, in the first half of the thirteenth century, a remarkable change appears to come about in the theory of fortification in Wales and the March. Mottes and baileys were still being built in the reign of King John, two new ones apparently being constructed (or reconstructed) at Builth Wells in 1210 and Mathrafal in 1212. These could have been the last mottes built in England and Wales (but apparently not in Ireland or on the Continent). In their place, during the reign of Henry III, impressive stone citadels were built on great crags, possibly in the Poitou mould. Thus, in 1223, a new castle was founded at Montgomery on a virgin elevated position, echoed by the earl of Chester's new rock fortress of Beeston begun around 1225. Of the new royal castles built at this time Painscastle, in 1231, is the only exception to the rule, being a refortified motte and bailey, and not, like Henry III's other fortresses, on a highland site. On the death of Llywelyn Fawr in 1240 this new highland castle policy was carried through on a far greater scale, with the new castle of the rock being founded at Dyserth to replace the ancient motte and bailey of Robert of Rhuddlan which he built at the command of William the Conqueror between 1071 and 1075. Degannwy too was rebuilt on a massive scale destroying nearly all the evidence of the previous Norman stone castle. In the March of Wales these new castles appeared in some numbers in the lands controlled by the Mortimers, *viz.* at Cefnllys, Knucklas and Tinboeth.

However, as the native dynasties were never reduced to impotence or secured as vassals for any considerable period of time as happened in other parts of the March, it meant that the Norman conquest of this region was never really secure and that rapid and occasionally long-lasting native reconquest was a recurrent threat. As a consequence the castles in these insecure lands had a resilience and military relevance which their counterparts were fairly rapidly to lose in much of England. This continuing military threat meant that the March was constantly a scene of innovation, with the result that there are many castles with intriguing designs, some being innovative, others archaic and many that do not fit readily into any category.

The History of Radnorshire's castles

What are castles?

In the early Medieval period in Wales and the border up to 1282, castles in the true sense of the word, were for defence. Other buildings more like country houses were built where the primary function was living accommodation. Not surprisingly these lightly fortified houses were built away from the dangerous frontiers. It is noticeable too that in the Domesday Book there are references to enigmatic fortified houses as well as to castles. Such a distinction is obviously not just fanciful thinking. However, when it came to castles proper, the defensive quality of the building was paramount to a lord, his splendour in residence came second. In the early days lords were itinerant, moving from place to place with their increasingly large retinues and consuming the foodstuffs of the district at, for the local populace, an alarming rate. A lord could not stay in one place simply because of the cost to the local community. He would literally eat them out of house and home. In 1278, when Prince Llywelyn ap Gruffydd was in dispute with the Abbot of Basingwerk, there is an interesting list of what a lord expected from his vassals when he was in residence. Previously his uncle and grandfather, Dafydd ap Llywelyn and Llywelyn ab Iorwerth, had expected the abbot to provide for the prince's hunting parties of 300 men at his Boch–y–rhaiadr grange. Prince Llywelyn was now expecting them to entertain his retinue of 500 men and the abbot thought the increase in numbers unreasonable, the cost being some £8 annually. £8 then was a large sum when the average foot soldier only received 2d. a day—an annual wage of just over £3 a year. Manual labourers may have only earned half that amount. This graphically illustrates the costs of entertaining one's lord and provides one good reason why the lord's lives had to be itinerant.

Loyalty to the lord, especially in the early days, was strictly personal and if the lord did not show his face to his vassals often enough they could turn to another lord for protection and advancement. This problem was especially rife in the Marches of Wales when often several barons, Norman and Welsh, claimed the same piece of land. It was inevitable that most peasants would find life unbearable, being taxed by both sides to support the wars being fought over the lands they farmed. Consequently, loyalty in the Marches proved fickle. In some histories it is suggested that the tenants proved turncoats in their allegiance. This was not really so, most of them would support the lord in their region who was most powerful at that time rather than risk losing all in, what was to them, the vagaries of political warfare. Loyalty may have been cheap, but land was always worth holding on to. In this way, as the tenants looked to their lord for protection, the lord considered his peasants to be a source of income, rather like a dairy farmer regards his cattle today. If a village proved reluctant to obey him, it was far better to slaughter the lot, and suffer such loss of income from one village, than have the disobedience spread and lose all of his tenants. This view of rebellion was similar to that of an outbreak of foot and mouth disease today!

In this landscape the castle was a durable sign of authority. In December, 1256, Prince Llywelyn overran the cantref of Buellt, but could not take the castle. As a consequence, by Easter 1257, the castle garrison had brought the local Welsh back to their fealty to the Crown. Without the presence of Llywelyn the native inhabitants of the region were unable to withstand the domination of the castle. In January, 1259, Llywelyn returned and again occupied the land except for the castle. By 10 April of the same year Roger Mortimer of Wigmore had brought the cantref back to royal obedience and was sending 'malefactors' to Bridgnorth Castle for incarceration at the royal will. Once more the power of the castle to overawe a district is made plain. In January, 1260, Llywelyn yet again invaded the cantref and this time besieged the castle with siege engines. Once more Roger Mortimer raised the siege and brought the province back under English control by April. Finally, on 17 July, when Roger

The Castles of Radnorshire

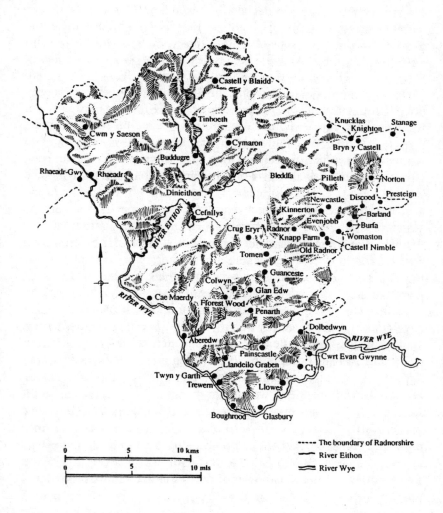

● Castell y Blaidd

● Tinboeth

Cwm y Saeson ●

● Cymaron

Buddugre ●

Rhaeadr-Gwy ● Rhaeadr ●

● Knucklas
Knighton ●
● Stanage

● Bryn y Castell

Bleddfa ●
● Pilleth
● Norton

Dinieithon ●

Cefnllys ●

Newcastle ●
Discoed ●
● Presteign

Kinnerton ●
● Barland

Crug Eryr ● Radnor ●
Evenjobb ●
● Burfa

Knapp Farm ●
● Womaston

Tomen ●
Old Radnor ●
Castell Nimble ●

RIVER EITHON

● Guanceste

Colwyn ●

Cae Maerdy ●
● Glan Edw

RIVER WYE
Fforest Wood ●

● Penarth

● Dolbedwyn
RIVER WYE

Aberedw ●
Painscastle ●
● Cwrt Evan Gwynne
Llandeilo Graben ●
● Clyro

Twyn y Garth ●
Trewern ●
● Llowes

Boughrood ●   ● Glasbury

0 ____ 5 ____ 10 kms
0 ____ 5 ____ 10 mls

----- The boundary of Radnorshire
—— River Eithon
≋ River Wye

15

Mortimer was in London, Buellt Castle was treacherously surrendered to the local Welsh and Rhys Fychan of Dinefwr demolished the castle so thoroughly that English rule ended in the district until 1276. Without the castle to dominate the land the task of subduing the district was too difficult and the cantref was abandoned as uneconomic until times had become more favourable for the invaders to re–assert their authority, rebuild the castle and dominate the district. The main purpose of the castle can therefore be seen to have been military. Accommodation on the frontier was of secondary interest to self–preservation, as it has always been. It was only later, with the pacification of a district, that the castle was abandoned, for new, cheaper and more homelike surroundings, for it was often far too costly and difficult to convert the cold, dark and forbidding fortresses into comfortable country residences. This is why we often find a manor house or farm adjacent to a castle ruin. But the old castle was still there just in case—a kind of insurance policy.

It can therefore be seen that a castle was primarily a military structure, occupied by its masters on their continual perambulation of their territories. When the lord was not in residence the castle was looked after by a constable and one or two paid soldiers. In time of war the garrison would rapidly be augmented by the local populace and landholders who owed military service at the castle to their lord for the privilege of holding their lands. This may seem haphazard today, but at that time it was impossible to move a large attacking force quickly, therefore a castle garrison had time to form the defence. Generally the feudal military land obligation was a period of service at the landowner's own cost, sometimes in person, sometimes by a certain number of knights, mounted infantry, bowmen or footmen for a set number of days. Initially the service was for 40 days, but as these fees, as they were called, were split amongst co–heirs the amount of service would diminish and by the thirteenth century many obligations were down to a few days. For a lord wishing to undertake military operations such a piecemeal and part–time army was obviously less than satisfactory, and so as time went by military obligations tended to be relinquished in place of a cash payment, so that a lord could hire professional armed forces who would fight whilst pay was forthcoming and not go home at times of vital need simply because the length of service they owed to their lord was expended.

The castles of Radnorshire are primarily fighting castles. Few if any were built with comfort or accommodation in mind, although Cefnllys, for example, saw many subsequent rebuildings which made it a fit home for a fourteenth century dowager countess. The bloody campaigns that will be related below clearly show the changing military designs over two hundred years of nearly continuous warfare, when this land was the Middle March of Wales.

Castles were not built to any pre–conceived rigid plan, rather they took advantage of any existing defensive features. They are often found at the end of ridges, on hilltops, at the junction of rivers or in marshy ground, all of which offered immediate advantages to the defender. Once the position had been chosen, elements were then added to make the defensive attributes of the site greater. A large ditch might be dug and powerful ramparts built with the resultant spoil. Often a huge mound of earth called a motte would be made. Timber works might be built on or in these earthen defences, sometimes a palisade round the edge of the ditch and on top of the rampart. Then a wooden tower might be built on or, in several cases, within the motte.

In Radnorshire many castles are of the type called motte and bailey, that is the large steep–sided conical mound with a defensive enclosure at its base. Later, or sometimes simultaneously with these constructions, stone elements were added to the castle. Sometimes a stone gateway, the most vulnerable part of the castle, sometimes a stone tower on or in the motte and nearly always at some time in a castle's life, wooden or stone accommodation was added in the bailey. The lack of such accommodation could well prove disastrous for the garrison, especially in a bleak winter such as that at Cefnllys in the campaign of 1262.

Pre–Norman Radnorshire, Commotes and Cantrefs

Although castles had been constructed in Herefordshire since the late Saxon period when a Norman earl had been installed in the county, there is no direct evidence of any in Radnorshire until well into the reign of William the Conqueror (1066–87). Before the Norman Conquest the part of the country that was to become

Radnorshire was divided into various land units called cantrefs which are rough equivalents of English shires. Similarly, like their English counterparts, the larger units were subdivided into three or four commotes which were the smallest units of justice. Just as in England service was owed to the Hundred Court, in Wales it was owed to the commotal court or llys. Consequently, when the Normans invaded Wales, they used the commote as the unit of penetration in a manner similar to the way they had absorbed England. In Wales the lord of a commote was a man of great importance and was apparently called a king, although he may have owed allegiance to his neighbours who were more powerful. The situation has been rightly compared to a crazy jigsaw puzzle of interlocking and overlapping spheres of influence, each a kingdom in its own right. Such laissez-faire confusion was anathema to the orderly-minded feudal barons which characterised the Normans. Their objectives of defining their lands, if possible at a neighbour's cost, helped lead to those indeterminable wars for which border regions throughout the world are renowned.

The Norman arrival in Wales, 1067–1087

Little has been recorded of the Normans' early thrusts into Wales. What we do know of Radnorshire is much buttressed by occurrences in other shires. The first Norman to attempt to hold sway over this district was William fitz Osbern, William the Conqueror's first earl of Hereford. It seems unlikely that Earl William was in Herefordshire before 1068 due to the turbulence of the realm. In 1068 and 1069 severe fighting against an alliance of the Saxons and Welsh was occurring in Cheshire, Shropshire and northern Herefordshire. This forced Earl William to relieve the besieged Norman garrison of Shrewsbury in the desperate campaign of 1069. Finally, in 1070, the earl turned against the Welsh who had aided the rebellious Saxons and in the summer defeated three Welsh kings in Brycheiniog[1]. This victory gave Earl William a foothold in Wales and he strengthened this transitory military victory by building castles along the frontier at Wigmore, Clifford, Monmouth

1. Rhys [ab Owain], Cadwgan [ap Meurig] and Maredudd [ab Owain], all three kings probably being of the kingdom of Deheubarth, or South Wales as it would have been called by the English.

and Chepstow, as well as rebuilding the earlier fortress at Ewias Harold. He was probably also responsible for founding the first castle at New Radnor for, according to the Domesday Book, he was the lord of the Radnor Plain and lordship in the Early Middle Ages almost always implied the dominating presence of a castle! It is almost certain that a swathe of other castles were founded simultaneously by other minor lords in the wake of the great earl. Thus some ten minor castles were built around Wigmore Castle by knights enfeoffed of the land to hold it by military service. Such military service can also probably be applied to some of the motte castles in the Radnor Plain. Research may well show further minor castles supporting the other castles at Clifford, Monmouth and Chepstow. However, before the famous earl could capitalize on his successes he was killed on 22 February, 1071, in a battle in Flanders where he was trying to obtain his inheritance. This shows an earl of cosmopolitan European culture more at home with lords of Western Christendom than amongst his own native serfs.

In Wales the death of Earl William led to the devolution of his lordship upon the shoulders of his son Roger, who became the second post–Conquest earl of Hereford. Earl Roger continued the consolidation of the Welsh Marches finishing the construction of Monmouth Castle by having a chapel consecrated in it, to which service was invited his father's old foe, King Cadwgan ap Meurig. Earl Roger did not prove as successful a baron as his father and in 1075 was dispossessed of his lands after an abortive rebellion, aided by his Welsh vassals, against the Conqueror. It was in the aftermath of this event that Ralph Mortimer (d.1135+) was installed at Wigmore Castle on the Radnorshire March. To the south, at New Radnor, the land and probably the earl's castle were taken into the king's hands, despite the objection of Hugh the Ass (this was a compliment as the stubbornness of an ass was seen as a virtue) of nearby Knighton and Norton. He claimed that Radnor had been granted to him by Earl William!

By Domesday (1086) Hugh the Ass, who was an ancestor of the Chandos family of Snodhill, was recorded as holding the vills of Knighton and Norton in Radnorshire together with a great forest. All was waste when Hugh took over and it was still waste in 1086. Similarly, his neighbour, Ralph Mortimer, held Pilleth, part of

Harpton and Weston[1] in Radnorshire, whilst another neighbour Osbern fitz Richard of Richard's Castle, held Cascope, part of Harpton, Discoed and Knill. All these lands were classified as waste and were worth nothing to the lords who held them, other than the pleasure that could be had from the hunting. Although the land was waste and was worth nothing in revenue it did not mean that there were no castles there. On the contrary, a mention in Domesday suggests that there was a possibility of revenue being gained from the lands. The Domesday Book was not a royal attempt to list the contents of the country with the landholders and their fees, it was more of a giant tax inquisition by an oppressive king, eager to tax his subjects to bulwark his army against an expected invasion of the kingdom from Scandinavia. As today some people may fiddle their tax returns, so too at the time of Domesday it is likely that those returning their landholdings might have been economical with the truth, especially in the border areas where landholdings were uncertain and sudden expenses for warfare might occur at any time. Certainly the Domesday inspectors seem to have paid little heed to Wales, ignoring most Norman and friendly Welsh held lands to the west of the present border. Charter, coin and chronicle evidence suggests that the Norman penetration included Cardiff, St Davids, Abergavenny (all three held by the king), Brecon (earls of Hereford, then Neufmarché), Rhuddlan, Degannwy and Bangor (all three held under the earl of Chester), yet no mention is made of these lands in the survey. The most probable reason for this omission is that these lands in newly conquered territories were sources of expenditure rather than income, so they were of no interest to the surveyors who were only interested in tax revenue.

However, the Domesday Book does throw some much needed light on the rulers of contemporary Radnorshire. One entry in the Herefordshire section states that Rhys ap Tewdwr of Deheubarth owed the king £40 per annum for South Wales, in the same manner as Robert of Rhuddlan owed the king £40 for North Wales. Further, the land of Cynllibiwg (Saint Cynllo's land as it has been alleged, or Rhwng Gwy a Hafren, the land between the Wye and the Severn, as it is now known), paid 10s. to the revenue of Herefordshire. This strongly suggests that the bulk of Radnorshire, apart from the few

1. The llys of Swydd Rhiwallt?

Norman-held vills on the border that have been mentioned above, was held by their native lords. This was almost certainly the descendants of Cadwgan the son of Elystan Glodrydd, the king of Central Wales, supposedly killed near Kerry or Ceri in present day Montgomeryshire in 1010.

The Norman Conquest and Consolidation of Radnorshire 1088–1134

The principal Norman conquest of South Wales dates to the time after the crushing of the revolt of the border barons, Ralph Mortimer, Richard fitz Scrope and Bernard Neufmarché and their Welsh allies and tenants in the summer of 1088. Soon reconciled with King William Rufus who came to the throne in 1087, they returned to their Marches where fortune was soon to favour their cause. In April, 1093, Bernard Neufmarché was constructing a castle at Brecon when the king of South Wales, Rhys ap Tewdwr, marched his army into Brycheiniog only to be met, defeated and killed by Bernard. This defeat opened the flood gates to the Norman advance and rapidly Pembroke, Carmarthen, Ceredigion, Arwystli and, encircled by the above mentioned areas, Radnorshire, were overrun. The cantref of Maelienydd was taken by Ralph Mortimer of Wigmore and two commotes of the cantref of Elfael were taken by Ralph Tosny of Clifford. The third commote of Elfael, Radnor or Llythyfnwg as it may then have been known was, about that time, granted by the king to William Braose (d.c.1094) or more likely to his son and heir Philip (d.c.1138), the forefathers of one of the great Marcher houses.

This arbitrary military absorption of the independent areas of the Welsh March was to strongly influence the politics of the succeeding two centuries. In the period 1098–1101 the Archbishop of Canterbury wrote to Ralph Mortimer, Bernard Neufmarché, Philip Braose and others complaining of their seizure of lands in the diocese of St Davids. One must wonder why he did not also complain of Ralph Tosny who most certainly was holding Elfael, another part of the diocese, unless it had been successfully attached to either the sees of Hereford or Llandaff, both of which had laid claim to it.

What happened to the descendants of Elystan Glodrydd during this period is uncertain. Two, Ifor and Gruffydd ab Idnerth, were

21

The Marcher Campaign of 1093

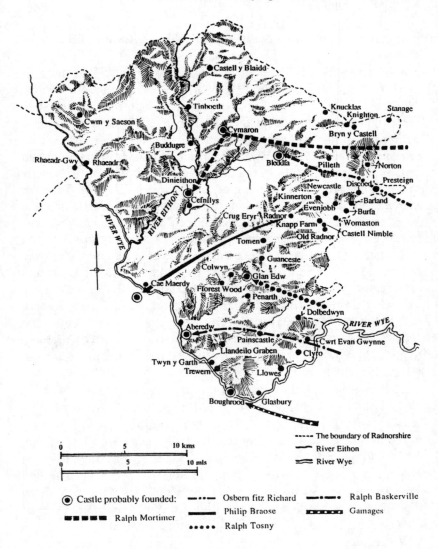

Castell y Blaidd

Tinboeth

Knucklas
Knighton   Stanage

Cwm y Saeson

Cymaron

Bryn y Castell

Buddugre

Rhaeadr-Gwy   Rhaeadr

Bleddfa

Pilleth   Norton

Dinieithon

Newcastle   Discoed   Presteign

RIVER EITHON

Cefnllys

Kinnerton   Barland

Crug Eryr   Radnor   Evenjobb   Burfa

Knapp Farm   Womaston

RIVER WYE

Tomen   Old Radnor   Castell Nimble

Colwyn   Guanceste

Glan Edw

Fforest Wood

Penarth

Cae Maerdy

Dolbedwyn

RIVER WYE

Aberedw

Painscastle   Cwrt Evan Gwynne

Llandeilo Graben   Clyro

Twyn y Garth

Trewern   Llowes

Boughrood   Glasbury

-----	The boundary of Radnorshire
———	River Eithon
≡≡≡	River Wye

Scale:
0   5   10 kms
0   5   10 mls

Castle probably founded: ·-·-·- Osbern fitz Richard   -·-·- Ralph Baskerville
■■■■■ Ralph Mortimer   ——— Philip Braose   ◻◻◻◻ Gamages
                                ····· Ralph Tosny

22

opposing the Normans in Brycheiniog in 1096. Their uncle meanwhile seems to have held lands in Herefordshire as the official interpreter between the Normans and Welsh. He appeared as Llywelyn Latimer in Domesday and was killed in Brycheiniog in 1099, though whether by the Normans or Welsh is not stated. Before his death he appears to have been in charge of the royal mint at Carmarthen where coins were issued with the inscription 'Llywelyn ap Cadwgan, Rex'. It would therefore seem that Llywelyn reached his position in society as an Anglophile, just as other members of his family were to do later.

The general Welsh war ground to a halt in 1099 and set the scene in Wales for the forceful reign of Henry I. King Henry (1100–35) ruled Wales with an iron fist and several of the Marcher lords were to feel his displeasure. Philip Braose of Radnor and Buellt was dispossessed between 1110 and 1112. Geoffrey, the son and heir of Bernard Neufmarché, was dispossessed on a technicality around 1128 and Brecon was granted to Miles of Gloucester, one of Henry's staunchest supporters. Ralph Tosny also fell foul of the king and was dispossessed of his lands and his son was in prison when Henry I died in December, 1135. In Radnorshire, Elfael at the time was probably held by another of the king's trusted servants, Pain fitz John (d.1137) after whom Painscastle is almost certainly named. Pain also seems to have acquired Maelienydd on the expulsion of Ralph Mortimer from the kingdom either in 1118/9 or 1127/8 when his son-in-law, Stephen of Aumale, led rebellions against the king. By the end of Henry's reign custody of most of the Middle March, and nearly all of Radnorshire, lay in the hands of the king's able lieutenant, Pain fitz John, also known as Pain Monoculus, or 'one-eyed'.

Although the slight documentary evidence seems to suggest that the Normans had it all their own way in the early conquest of Radnorshire there are two sources that suggest a Welsh princely influence did continue in Maelienydd at least. A contemporary panegyric suggests that Hywel ap Goronwy ap Cadwgan had reoccupied 'in pledge' Ewias, Ergyng, Gwent, Morgannwg, the valley of the Monnow (Monmouth), Penrhin (in Narberth), Ystrad Tywi, Garway, Dyfed of the two Dominions (possibly Norman French and Welsh), Cardigan and a part of Maelienydd, but that he could not obtain Brycheiniog which was 'of his just inheritance'. The poem further claimed that Ystrad Tywi and Rhydygors had both been 'entrusted' to Hywel and although Ceri, Elfael and Buellt are all mentioned Hywel is not claimed to have any influence in them, suggesting that they were then Norman held. The fact that the above two lands were held in trust indicates that the poem was written probably in the period 1102 to 1105 when Hywel was granted lands by Henry I and appears high in royal favour. Hywel was killed by the Normans with the aid of his son's foster father in 1106. Then in 1109 the men of Maelienydd, possibly independent of Mortimer rule, took the part of Henry I's officers against the rebel Welsh of Powys and Ceredigion.

What little independence the Welsh of Radnorshire had during the reign of Henry I was dramatically increased in the anarchy that followed his death.

The National Revival 1135 to 1194

Even before King Henry's death on 1 December, 1135, trouble was afoot in Wales. Three times the king tried to leave Normandy to deal with the growing revolt in the west, and three times events thwarted him, until finally death overtook him after eating the famous 'surfeit of lampreys' for tea. Up until then the revolt in Wales was restricted to the Welsh of the Middle March, with Ralph Mortimer's old castle of Cymaron, which was then under the care of Pain fitz John, being burned and the garrison put to the sword. With Henry's death the revolt gathered pace and in October, 1136, on Black Monday as it became known to the 3,000 widows of the Norman soldiery, a united Welsh army destroyed a Marcher army at the battle of Cardigan. Prominent in the action both before and after the event was Madog ab Idnerth, the leading Welsh lord of Maelienydd. But Madog did not live long enough to capitalize on his victory, for he died in 1140, about the same time that Hugh Mortimer, the son of Ralph, was restored to Wigmore by King Stephen. Hugh's reinstatement had no doubt been hastened by the removal of Pain fitz John Monoculus from the scene, run through the head by a lance while chasing a Welsh raiding party on 10 July, 1137.

The reign of King Stephen proved a disaster for Wales. Stephen successfully usurped the English throne after the death of his uncle

Henry I, on the grounds that the kingdom should not be inherited by a woman, the Empress Matilda being the only direct heir of Henry. For 3 years the state of the kingdom gradually deteriorated as the barons discovered, as one English chronicler put it, that Stephen was 'soft'. The result was a civil war between Stephen and the supporters of the Empress who, after her marriage to Geoffrey of Anjou, came to be known as Angevins.

Soon after Madog ab Idnerth's death his two sons, Maredudd and Cadwgan appeared with their troops, together with the Angevin Earls of Chester and Gloucester, before the besieged Lincoln Castle on 2 February, 1141. There they were met by King Stephen and Hugh Mortimer's nephew, Earl William of Aumale and one of the major battles of the English realm then occurred. Maredudd's and Cadwgan's unarmoured troops were scattered in the first assault, but their rout gave time for the main Angevin forces to close and destroy the royal army. King Stephen, fighting with the madness of desperation, was cornered and after a valiant struggle overthrown. The two Welsh princes did not live long to savour their allies' triumph, bought at the expense of their mens' blood. In 1142 Cadwgan and another brother, Hywel, were killed by the 'contrivance' of Helias Say the royalist lord of Clun, who had annexed large areas of the brothers' lands around Bleddfa. Two years later Hugh Mortimer marched into Radnorshire and rebuilt the castles of Cymaron and Colwyn and, according to the Welsh Chronicles, 'for a second time the French conquered Maelienydd and Elfael'. (The Welsh often referred to the Normans as 'the French'.) Hugh Mortimer, an ardent royalist, seems to have had more in mind than merely re-occupying his father's and the Tosnys' lands. He was also threatening from the north the Angevin Miles of Gloucester's ill-gotten gains at Brecon.

Hugh Mortimer continued his campaigns in Radnorshire over the next few years. In 1145, he captured Rhys ap Hywel of Brycheiniog after killing some of his men and capturing others. The next year the royalists gained their final vengeance for the battle of Lincoln when Hugh settled his score with Maredudd ap Madog. 1147 saw the high point of royalist advance in the west when Hugh blinded Rhys ap Hywel in his prison. From here on events went steadily downhill. The royalist bishop of Hereford died in 1148 and Hugh seized his castle of Ledbury North (Bishop's Castle) and his ally, the Earl of Mellent and Worcester, seized the other castle of the see. The new bishop threw his support behind Roger, the Angevin Earl of Hereford, and he and Joce Dinan of Ludlow began to pin Hugh Mortimer back into his castles. During this period Hugh was captured by Joce and ransomed for 3,000 marks and all his precious metals. It was probably during his period of confinement that Maelienydd and Elfael fell from his grasp. Certainly when they are next mentioned, in 1163, they were in the hands of Cadwallon and Einion Clud, the only surviving sons of Madog ab Idnerth.

The civil war, or Anarchy as it is better known, wound on its bloody way until the death of Stephen's eldest son and heir, Prince Eustace, in 1153. He subsequently signed a peace treaty with the young Henry Plantagenet of Anjou, Matilda's son, soon to be proclaimed Henry II of England. Hugh Mortimer had certainly come to terms with the future king by September, 1153, and it is to be presumed that his enemies in Wales would have been allowed to keep their lands, especially considering the service they had rendered the Angevin cause at Lincoln and elsewhere.

In 1160, Cadwallon ap Madog seized his brother Einion Clud and sent him a prisoner to Owain Gwynedd, King of North Wales, who in turn transferred Einion to his lord, Henry II. The very same year Einion was allowed to escape from his Worcester prison and Cadwallon paid his first fine to the Crown. Obviously the Crown recognized Cadwallon as lord of his lands in Central Wales. In 1163 King Henry marched an army through South Wales in a bloodless campaign and returned to Hereford via Radnorshire, crossing the commotes of Deuddwr, Maelienydd and Radnor. Two years later Henry invaded North Wales, this time being repulsed by the united army of Wales at Corwen in the Berwyn mountains of Powys. Two of the leaders of the Welsh army were Cadwallon and Einion Clud. Whilst these two princes were away Hugh Mortimer invaded Radnorshire in yet another attempt to regain what he deemed were his lost ancestral lands. Henry II, enraged at this continuance of a private war without royal sanction, slapped a hefty fine on Mortimer. This was recorded at the royal exchequer for the next 100 years, but never paid, apart from a few token shillings.

In 1170, fighting broke out between the Prince of Elfael and the princes of Gwent which resulted in Einion Clud being wounded by Meilyr and Ifor, the sons of Llywarch ap Dyfnwal. War also raged against the Normans in the March. On 29 June, 1175, King Henry called all the combatants, English, Welsh and Norman, before him at Gloucester and there rubber-stamped the *status quo*, much to the annoyance of the Marcher lords and in particular Hugh Mortimer of Wigmore who was much distrusted by the king. In recompense for the royal recognition of their lands the princely brothers of Radnorshire pledged 500 marks (£333 6s. 8d.) to the Crown—the self-same amount that Hugh Mortimer had been fined in 1165. Like their Marcher counterpart the brothers paid little of their fine, but this was not through intransigence, merely the hand of death. In 1176, Cadwallon capitalized on his newly won peace and founded the Cistercian Abbey Cwmhir deep inside his own territories. The next year Einion Clud was killed by unrecorded assassins and Cadwallon seized all his brother's lands and was recorded in England that year as Cadwallon, King of Elfael. Radnorshire was now almost totally in Cadwallon's hands. The only parts beyond his grasp were New Radnor and the associated castles in the plain between there and the hills before Kington and the border vills of Knighton and Norton, now held by the Chandos family as the heirs of Hugh the Ass. However, the same year as Cadwallon and his western neighbour, Rhys ap Gruffydd of Deheubarth, were in England meeting the king, Prince Rhys was having a castle built at Rhaeadr-gwy in Radnorshire on the west side of the Wye. This fortress was to prove a cause of dissension between the two and their heirs for many years to come.

If Cadwallon thought he had built himself a little kingdom to rule peacefully in his aging years he was wrong. In September, 1179, he had to venture to the king's court to defend himself over charges brought against him, probably concerning his rule in Elfael. On his return, on 22 September, he was set upon by the adherents of the young Roger Mortimer of Wigmore and slain. If Roger, who, unlike his father, was in high favour with the king, thought to gain by this deed he was cruelly mistaken. Instead of gaining a kingdom he found himself in the king's prison at Winchester for two years. Some of his men were imprisoned and others faced outlawry, so great was the king's ire. In Elfael the sons of Einion Clud now took the place of their uncle and in Maelienydd Cadwallon's sons ruled jointly, but the strength of the kingdom Cadwallon had slowly and painfully built up in Radnorshire was badly shaken. Its death throes would last for the next 20 years.

If the Mortimer clan had intended the death of Cadwallon to be the prelude to the easy annexation of Radnorshire they were sadly disappointed. With the lord of the land dead, Henry II's sheriff of Herefordshire, Ralph le Poer, marched into Maelienydd and took charge of Cymaron Castle and the surrounding district for the Crown as Cadwallon, a tenant–in–chief, had died greatly in debt to the king. For the next three years royal forces held the castle against an increasingly hostile population. The end came in 1182. The Welsh of the Middle March, smarting under the rule of William Braose, the most powerful Marcher in Wales and Ralph le Poer, King Henry's blood-thirsty sheriff, revolted under the direction of Rhys ap Gruffydd of Deheubarth. William and Ralph with their combined army were routed at Dingestow near Monmouth, where they were trying to build a castle and in quick succession Cymaron, Radnor and Abergavenny castles were seized by the rebels. The king was out of the kingdom at the time and the Justiciar had to march west to try to stem the flow, but little could be done other than strengthening the remaining castles and releasing Roger Mortimer from his sojourn at Winchester. In July, 1184, King Henry called Rhys ap Gruffydd to Gloucester and there Rhys promised the king that he would return the castles he had seized in Radnorshire and elsewhere. However, he later reneged on his promise, stating that those holding the castles refused to relinquish them. These men were undoubtedly the sons of Cadwallon and Einion Clud.

The status of the Welsh advance in Radnorshire was shown in early March, 1188, when the Archbishop of Canterbury and Giraldus Cambrensis perambulated the principalities preaching the crusade. They entered Wales from Hereford at Radnor where they met Prince Einion o'r Porth of Elfael, the son of Einion Clud. Soon afterwards Einion's father–in–law, Rhys ap Gruffydd of Deheubarth, joined them. From New Radnor the party moved to Castell Crug Eryr where they were met by Maelgwn ap Cadwallon,

28

the Prince of Maelienydd. Both princes took the cross and so pledged to crusade in the Holy Land, though both found reasons to disavow their oath. On 6 July, 1189, Henry II died and the peace that had ruled in Radnorshire for the last 5 years or so dissolved. Rhys ap Gruffydd brought warfare into Pembroke and Carmarthen, while the Princes of Radnorshire reverted to the internecine wars that had so damaged that area in the past. Prince John probably entertained them at Worcester around 1 September and stirred up the rivalries between them. John, himself a Marcher through marriage and one time lord of Ireland, knew well the doctrine of divide and rule! Early in 1191, Einion o'r Porth was struck down by one of his brothers and Giraldus spoke of bloody and abhorrent deeds occurring in the territories lying between the Wye and the Severn. In 1193, Einion o'r Porth's possible son and probable heir Anarawd, fighting no doubt for his very survival against his uncles, seized his brothers Madog and Hywel and had their eyes gouged out. Meanwhile his uncle, Iorwerth Clud, was in the pay of the Earl Marshall fighting against Prince John and his Welsh allies, one of whom may have been Anarawd! In 1194 Rhys ap Gruffydd rebuilt his castle at Rhaeadr-gwy and it was promptly destroyed by Maelgwn ap Cadwallon and his brothers, who had previously destroyed it! It must have been with increasing glee that the great border families of Mortimer and Braose looked on as the Welsh of Radnorshire tore themselves to pieces and waited for the moment to reap the fruits of their traditional enemies' self-inflicted wounds.

The Marcher Conquest 1195–1214

The long awaited settling of old scores began in 1195, though few would probably have believed that the war would drag on for five long years. Under the aegis of the government of Richard the Lion Heart, who had paid his second and final fleeting visit to his kingdom, the Marchers of South Wales attacked. Roger Mortimer with the levy of Herefordshire and Worcestershire marched on Cymaron Castle and expelled the sons of Cadwallon. The redoubtable Maud Braose closed in on Painscastle where she was credited with 'slaughtering the Welsh'. Her husband stormed St Clears in Carmarthenshire and the sons of Rhys ap Gruffydd joined in the fray seizing castles and plundering the land. The next year, his

The Campaign of 1196

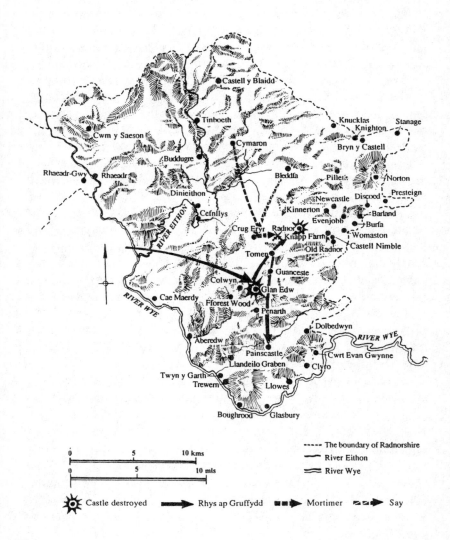

Castle destroyed   Rhys ap Gruffydd   Mortimer   Say

---- The boundary of Radnorshire
— River Eithon
≈ River Wye

family problems solved by the imprisonment of two of his sons, the Lord Rhys assumed the offensive and after attacking Carmarthen his armies poured into Radnorshire and made for Colwyn Castle in upper Elfael. In a short while his forces overwhelmed the castle which was then burned. Rhys then pushed on to the east and sacked Radnor and stormed the castle. Meanwhile Roger Mortimer of Wigmore and Hugh Say of Richard's Castle had formed their army and were marching south from their bases at Cymaron and Bleddfa when they saw the flames of burning Radnor. Turning east to investigate they ran smack into the rear of the main forces of Rhys ap Gruffydd. Each side was facing its homelands down a steep–sided valley, and therefore to the loser, being forced to retreat into hostile territory, went the threat of annihilation. Unfortunately for the Marchers the day went against them to the alleged tune of 40 knights and an innumerable number of foot. The victory might have proved the saviour of independent Radnorshire but, on 28 April, 1197, in his moment of triumph the Lord Rhys was struck down by the plague that was then ravishing the country. Soon afterwards Maelgwn ap Cadwallon followed him to the grave, probably through similar circumstances. Bereft of strong leadership the end could not be long postponed. The Marchers, finally scenting victory, pushed on as the sons of Rhys began to fight bitterly amongst one another for the diminishing spoils of their father's principality.

The next year proved crucial to the Marcher cause. Roger Mortimer had by now succeeded in gaining control of the bulk of Maelienydd and many of the monks of Cwmhir fled to Cymer in North Wales to avoid the victors. Then in July, the divided and mutually hostile princelings of Radnorshire finally found another protector. Gwenwynwyn of South Powys moved southwards gathering the Welsh of the Marches to his cause. Around 22 July, reinforced with a body of Llywelyn ab Iorwerth's household troops, he began to besiege Painscastle in Elfael—to the astonishment of the age deigning to use either siege engines or catapults. Once more the Justiciar of an absent king gathered his forces to meet the challenge, while the troops of William Braose in the castle held desperately to their ramparts. On 13 August, the English host led by Geoffrey fitz Peter marched north from Hay on Wye, meeting the Welsh host on the same day and shattered it in the most crushing of victories[1]. The chroniclers speak of over 3,000 Welsh casualties and even today bones of the fallen are uncovered during ploughing or road widening operations to the south of the castle. The defeat was total and independent native rule in the Middle Marches was crushed for a generation.

On 1 March, 1200, Roger Mortimer made a charter defining the limits of the lands of Abbey Cwmhir. This was made for Roger's love of his family 'and all the men who had fallen in the conquest of Maelienydd'. With this final act complete, his enemies fled to Gwynedd or, submissive before Roger, left the kingdom to help King John with his continental problems. In Normandy, John granted a concession to William Braose that he might conquer what he could from the Welsh to increase his barony of Radnor. This was probably a licence, if he really needed one, to annex the old Tosny lands to the south of Radnor. In spite of this licence things did not go all the Marchers' way, for in July, 1202, Roger Mortimer was recalled from Normandy when 'the Welsh', after a fortnight's siege, took his castle of Gwrtheyrnion. After this a period of obscurity covers the affairs of Radnorshire for many years, as the Normans began to slowly convert the native population into English ways. The commotes of Maelienydd were changed into hundreds and disloyal native chiefs were replaced by trusted tenants like the Savage family of Shropshire. Even so, many native Welsh chiefs prospered under the strict, but ordered rule of the Marchers.

The troubles that occurred now tended to be between king and Marcher lords and in 1207 a dispute between William Braose and King John led to a full scale war which continued on and off until William fled the country in 1210. The action saw Knighton, Norton, Kington, Radnor and Painscastle seized by the Crown, although only Radnor and Kington were given royal garrisons; Knighton and Norton were transferred, first to Roger Mortimer and then to the sheriff of Shropshire, whilst Painscastle and Colwyn may have been given to one of the numerous mutually hostile

---

1. Amongst the slain were found Anarawd ab Einion of Elfael, Owain Rascop ap Cadwallon, the brother of Maelgwn of Maelienydd, Rhiryd ab Iestyn and Rhobert ap Hywel, Gwenwynwyn's lord of Cedewain. Further, Maredudd ap Cynan of Meirionydd was captured.

descendants of Einion Clud. In 1208 and 1210 the sheriff of Gloucester invaded Elfael from the south and may well have built a series of castles along the River Wye, one of which was in Radnorshire. He also appears to have fought against Iorwerth Clud who may have been holding the Aberedw area of Elfael at this time. However, all these internecine wars amongst the Normans now had the same effect on the Welsh as their own bloody feuds had done on the Marcher lords twenty years before—the tide was about to turn.

The Rule of Llywelyn ab Iorwerth 1212–40

Even before the collapse of the authority of King John, the Welsh of the Middle March began to agitate against the Marcher lords under the auspices of Llywelyn the Great of Gwynedd. Sometime between 1210 and 1212 Llywelyn wrote to his cousin Madog ap Maelgwn of Maelienydd and his relations who were then waging war against the king from Ceri, then a part of Maelienydd, now in Montgomeryshire. Llywelyn asked his cousin and friend Madog as well as his brothers and others[1] to desist in their attacks on Ratlinghope Priory for Llywelyn's love of his relations, the Corbets. The great fight back had already begun. Sometime between August, 1211, and July, 1212, Madog ap Maelgwn seems to have declared his independence in Maelienydd and granted lands in the Lugg Valley to Abbey Cwmhir. Unfortunately Madog seems to have gone too far and around 4 August, 1212, King John hanged Madog, his uncle Hywel ap Cadwallon and his cousin, Meurig Barrach ab Ieuaf of Maelienydd, at Bridgnorth. This pruning of the princely tree of Maelienydd brought some peace to Radnorshire, but could not hold back the storm clouds for long.

In early July, 1214, Roger Mortimer fell mortally ill and wrote to King John and his eldest son Hugh, who was serving the king in Poitou, asking to set down the burden of his lands upon his son. King John assented to the request on 10 July, not knowing that

---

1. Hywel ap Cadwallon, Maredudd ap Robert of Cedewain, Iorwerth Goch of Gwrtheyrnion and Meurig his brother and all his sons, Iorwerth Clud and Maredudd the sons of Einion Clud of Elfael and Iorwerth ap Meirion, a chief of Maelienydd who had earlier served under Roger Mortimer, and all their allies in Ceri.

Roger had died two days earlier. In the 'interregnum' that followed it can be assumed that the Welsh began to throw off the Mortimer yoke. On 18 December, King John, then in Monmouth due to the local disturbances, took Abbey Cwmhir under his personal protection. However, this did not greatly aid his new Marcher baron Hugh Mortimer or the royal administrators of the Braose lands in Radnorshire. On 15 May, 1215, Bishop Giles Braose of Hereford sent his younger brother Reginald to the Marches of Wales with orders to seize back the family estates now held by the Crown. In rapid succession the castles of Pencelli, Abergavenny, White Castle and Skenfrith fell into his hands. Then, when Giles himself arrived some little time later, Brecon, Radnor, Hay, Blaenllyfni and Buellt castles also came over to him. However, the castles of Colwyn and Painscastle in Elfael were left to Gwallter ab Einion Clud. It was obviously a shrewd step to allow the native Welsh their bit of glory in the opposition to King John. In the north of Radnorshire the Mortimers stood firm in their support of John, and Hugh stripped his Welsh lands bare of men and resources to aid the king against both the rebels and the French who were then invading southern England. While he was away the Braose family and their Welsh allies struck. They seized Cymaron Castle and demolished it and then with Llywelyn marched on Shrewsbury. On route they seized Knighton and Norton, before their advance was halted by the king's abject surrender at Runneymede on 15 June, 1215.

The destruction of Cymaron Castle ended Mortimer ambitions in Radnorshire for a whole generation. With the rebel Braose held territories to the south it was all that the Mortimer retainers could do to hold their own lands, their lord being absent with the main military force of the increasingly isolated King John. During the very mild December of 1215, the two remaining sons of Maelgwn of Maelienydd, Maredudd and Cadwallon, campaigned with their military strength alongside Llywelyn ab Iorwerth, storming their way through the desperately, but forlornly held castles of south-west Deheubarth. While the sons of Maelgwn gave their aid to their lord and protector of Gwynedd, Gwallter ab Einion Clud continued to consolidate his hold on Elfael, to the exclusion of his remaining brothers and their heirs. This he did with the connivance of King John who confirmed Gwallter in the holding of his lands when he returned to the royal fealty on 29 July, 1216. His Braose ex-masters did not return to their loyalty until 1217. This indicates that Gwallter must have successfully played the king off against a Marcher enemy. Divide and rule worked both ways. After performing his fealty, the new lord of Elfael probably accompanied his king and Hugh Mortimer north through Elfael, until on 2 August they came to Radnor, which had been abandoned by its Braose garrison and was consequently burned by a bitter, possibly already dying king.

With the crowning of a new king, Hugh Mortimer stayed loyal to the Crown and on 28 February, 1217, was with the royal army at Dorking. Meanwhile his lands in the Marches were being usurped by his enemies who now occupied the bulk of Radnorshire, even if Gwallter Clud did hold Elfael nominally for the Crown. On 23 June, Reginald Braose submitted to the new king, and was immediately attacked by his erstwhile Welsh allies. However, by November the war had finished and on 17 December Walter Clifford was ordered to bring Gwallter Clud back to the royal fealty. This no doubt meant that he was forced to do homage to Reginald Braose for Elfael, certainly he failed to retain total independence in the lands, and a token surrender was better than a war to the finish against impossible odds. In the aftermath of the war the regent of the child king, Henry III, ordered a survey to be made of Herefordshire which indicates that the Welsh had pushed the Marcher lords back virtually along the whole frontier, and that the Marchers had compensated for this loss by withdrawing what had previously been shire land of Herefordshire out of royal jurisdiction and into the March. The Welsh border now ran from Brilley up along the Elfael border, including all of St Michael with Brilley and Gladestry up to the Red Ditch above Radnor and from there to the Lugg opposite Pilleth. It then cut across north Herefordshire to Lye and then up to Wigmore. It was noted that Presteign in the vale of Kington Barony had been removed from the Honour by Thomas Fraxino and that in many places itinerant justices no longer went into the land due to its illegal inclusion in the March.

Prince Llywelyn came to terms with the new government on 16 March, 1218, when his conquests were tacitly recognized, though the regency would not alienate any royal lands. Consequently the matter was effectively put on hold until the king came of age. As the king was only 9 this effectively meant victory for Llywelyn and to a lesser degree for his allies, the former princes of Maelienydd, who were by now no more than very minor lords owing homage to Llywelyn. However, this did not mean that the Marcher lords were totally impotent in the face of the prince. On 24 April, 1218, the regency confirmed the grant by the sheriff of Shropshire of the border vills of Knighton and Norton to Hugh Mortimer and on 25 May, ordered Llywelyn to vacate these lands. Llywelyn quite naturally refused and the dispute became something of a *cause célèbre* until it terminated when Llywelyn quitclaimed his rights in the vills, probably in early 1230 when his daughter Gwladys Ddu married Ralph Mortimer. (A quitclaim was a legal instrument by which a claim to land was passed from one person to another.) If control of Maelienydd was firmly in the hands of Llywelyn, the same could not be said of Radnor itself, or the occasionally appurtenant land of Elfael. On 7 March, 1219, Elfael was claimed from Reginald Braose by his young nephew John, who soon found himself buttressed by the powerful support of Llywelyn, who was most interested in pressurising his recalcitrant son-in-law Reginald. However, if Llywelyn could use the law against his enemies so too could the Marcher lords. On 10 May, 1220, Llywelyn replied to the regency that he refused to turn the land of Maelienydd, which he held in custody, over to Hugh Mortimer as he had been ordered, as the king only had the right to the homage of the nobles of the land and that homage had been done to Llywelyn who in turn had done homage to Henry III. Here it is clearly stated that as far as Llywelyn was concerned the descendants of the old princes of Cynllibiwg were now no more than his vassals, he himself being the prince of this part of Wales. This claim to paramountcy in Central Wales did little to impress the regent and on 19 May the sheriff of Shropshire was ordered to transfer the land of Maelienydd back to Hugh Mortimer, which it was claimed Llywelyn had returned to royal custody at the meeting at Shrewsbury! Llywelyn again wrote that he would not abandon his cousins of Maelienydd and hinted that any further royal or Mortimer intervention in the district would result in war. The matter was allowed to rest, but the simmering Marcher resentment did not die.

If Llywelyn had called the bluff of the Marchers and Crown over the holding of Maelienydd, Hugh Mortimer could still cause the prince troubles over his repeated claims to the land and launch those indeterminable border raids that kept the country destabilised and dissatisfied. Slowly the chieftains of the lands came to see that it was to their greater profit to be seen as partisans of the Crown rather than allies of Llywelyn. The greatest example of this is Gwenwynwyn and his son Gruffydd who, during the thirteenth century, became great Marcher lords rather than princes of Wales. Others in the Middle Marches like Hywel ap Meurig and his family improved their lot through support of the Marchers and later of the king when they had been brought to his notice. Meanwhile the power of Llywelyn proved too strong to dislodge the descendants of Cadwallon from Maelienydd, though Hugh Mortimer seems to have campaigned in the district repeatedly before his death at Reading in November, 1227.

The childless Hugh was succeeded by his brother Ralph, who too had his pretensions to Maelienydd. However, the tide had yet to turn. In 1228, another war blew up between Llywelyn and the king and in late September Llywelyn's forces, probably under the aegis of Gwallter Fychan's son, Roger Vaughan, took Elfael from the king, who was holding the land due to the capture of William Braose in the mountains of Ceri by Llywelyn. William Braose was released in February, 1229, for the sum of £2,000 and the land of Buellt, but Llywelyn also seems to have retained the homage of the Welsh of Elfael, and therefore effectively held all Radnorshire except for Radnor itself. Yet things were very different now from the days of the Lord Rhys. Then the princes of this district held their hereditary lands directly from the king, though they accepted Rhys' help in co—ordinating their attacks and more importantly their defence. Now they owed homage and allegiance to Llywelyn. Effectively they had been disenfranchised of their royal birthright, not by the Normans, but by the Prince of Gwynedd. From this position recovery proved impossible. Llywelyn however, was still growing in stature and before 1 May, 1230, he adopted the title of Prince of Aberffraw and Lord of Snowdon. His son and grandson would outdo him, adopting the title Prince of Wales and Lord of Snowdon. However, such proud boasts, while heartening his

37

supporters, alienated other princes who rightly knew their own kingly origins and hated his trumped up supremacy.

Llywelyn's grip on Elfael increased in 1230 when on 2 May, he hanged the land's Norman lord, William Braose, who had been caught in a dalliance with Llywelyn's wife, Princess Joan, the illegitimate daughter of King John. The king promptly seized William's lands, but Radnor was the only castle he garrisoned in Radnorshire, Colwyn and Painscastle were already beyond his grasp. Around 3 June, 1231, it appears that Llywelyn's envoys to the king were captured and beheaded at Montgomery, though on whose orders is not known. The Prince immediately took to the warpath and obtained a fiery revenge. Amongst many other acts Radnor was stormed, the town burned and the castle destroyed. Llywelyn was now lord of all Radnorshire. No single foothold remained for the king or Marchers. However, things did not go all Llywelyn's way. On 22 July, the king counterattacked and marched into Elfael. It was probably on the same day that a royal force under Walter Godardville, probably the custodian of Hay Castle, was almost destroyed near Hay with the aid of the monks of Cwmhir who were apparently acting at the behest of Llywelyn. Reginald fitz Richard Argenten, his brother, and three other nobles were captured and 300 knights killed. As a result the monks from the sumptuous buildings recently rebuilt by Llywelyn at Cwmhir were fined 300 marks to save their grange of Carnass from being burned down. About the same time King Henry's main army came to a halt at the burned out buildings of Painscastle where the king began to rebuild the shattered ruin. Llywelyn attacked his scouting parties and vicious, bloody actions were fought throughout Radnorshire. Henry remained at Painscastle watching his wonderful new structure rise until 22 September, when he returned to England, though not before naming his new fortress *Maugre Llewellyn*, the bad neighbour of Llywelyn. Llywelyn, however, had little to fear even though Elfael Is Mynydd, the southern half of Elfael, never again came into his hands, protected as it was by this new castle. Henry's campaign, although hopeless in bringing Llywelyn to heel, could not be said to have been a totally unsuccessful affair, even if it did in reality amount to very little for the expense undertaken. As one chronicler put it the king had built one new castle while Llywelyn had destroyed 10 others. Such costly 'victories' could do the Marcher cause little good. In early November the king's representatives met the council of Llywelyn at Colwyn in Elfael Uwch Mynydd and agreed a truce, Elfael from now on being split between them.

An uneasy peace now descended on Radnorshire, with the king feverishly cutting new roads to his castle at Painscastle for its better security. During the winter Llywelyn is said to have made inroads on the lands held by Richard of Cornwall in Wales and as a consequence Richard recaptured Radnor and began rebuilding the castle at his own expense after 12 March, 1233. Then, soon after 22 May, 1233, war broke out along the March, not with Llywelyn, but between the king and several of his Marcher barons. At first Llywelyn looked on as an interested bystander, but then, as he realised that there was profit in this for him, he threw his weight behind the rebels and during the winter months of 1233/34 his army proved unstoppable, and in January, 1234, for a second time in a generation the Prince of Gwynedd captured Shrewsbury. In the meantime the Welsh of Elfael under the command of Roger Vaughan ap Gwallter Clud once more swarmed south. This time ignoring the powerful royal fortress at Painscastle they besieged the tower at Pipton, which the king's constable, Henry Turbeville, was ordered to relieve on 25 September, 1233. This was in spite of the fact that Llywelyn's main force did not enter the fray until after 14 October. Perhaps the Welsh lords of Elfael could still operate with some independence of action, or was Llywelyn simply testing the water? Whichever, the fate of Pipton Castle is not recorded.

The long wars with Llywelyn were finally brought to an end by the truce of Brockton on 6 March, 1234, which tacitly, but not directly, recognized that Llywelyn could not be shifted from his conquests. It contained the statement that no new castles were to be built or ruined ones repaired by either side in the disputed lands. The disputed lands, however, were obviously in Llywelyn's seisin. The truce was renewed by both parties up to Llywelyn's death, but at no time had the king recognized that Llywelyn held Radnorshire by right. At the prince's death therefore, the lands had to be regained—the next war was already planned. Llywelyn knew what was intended and he attempted to do the best for his son who would obviously have to continue the fight with King Henry after

Llywelyn's death. In March, 1238, Llywelyn, knowing that not too much time remained to him, began to prepare the succession by having his underlords swear fealty to his son, Dafydd, as his successor. The king, knowing what this meant, forbade Llywelyn's barons to give the homage they owed to the Crown to Llywelyn's son. It is notable that named amongst these barons were Owain ap Maredudd and his young son Gruffydd of Elfael, Maredudd the last surviving son of Maelgwn of Maelienydd and Owain ap Hywel and his brother Cadwallon, Maredudd's nephews of Ceri. Also in the long list of Welsh barons was Llywelyn's grandson, Llywelyn ap Gruffydd, soon to play such an important part in the history of Radnorshire. Regardless of the king's order homage was duly paid to Dafydd on 17 October, 1238, after much to-ing and fro-ing between the two courts. On 10 April, 1240, Llywelyn died leaving Prince Dafydd ready to enter into his father's lands, apparently without opposition. The scene was well set for further tragedy.

Mortimer Triumphant 1240–56
Early in May, 1240, Prince Dafydd rushed south to meet his cousin Henry III and on 15 May entered into the Treaty of Gloucester. Under this he agreed to place the ownership of the disputed Marcher lands, of which Radnorshire was a part, before a panel of English and Welsh judges presided over by Otto, the Papal Legate. However, just as all looked favourable for a compromise, King Henry began to hand out the disputed lands, apparently before arbitration. It would seem that no formal agreement had been reached as to which lands were considered to be disputed. Obviously they were not recognized in the same way by the contending parties. Large areas of Carmarthen and Cardigan were seized by the Earl Marshall and on 3 June, the king wrote to the sheriff of Hereford ordering him to deliver to Ralph Mortimer seisin of Maelienydd, 'recently restored by the arbitration of the Norwegian bishop and his friends from Dafydd, once prince of North Wales', at Gloucester. However, there is no record of any such arbitration. Other lands which 'Llywelyn, now dead, had unjustly disseized' from the hands of their lords were likewise resumed by the Crown and re-granted to their previous English and Welsh owners. Prince Dafydd appears to have sulked in his fastnesses, largely ignoring

Henry's calls to proceed with the allotted arbitrations, except by attempting to have them postponed, and plotted his vengeance.

On 3 February, 1241, the magnates of Radnorshire began returning to their fealty to the king. First came Owain ab Iorwerth Clud and Owain ap Maredudd of Elfael to give homage at Hereford. Then at Lent, Owain ap Hywel, Maredudd ap Maelgwn, Hywel ap Cadwallon, Maredudd ap Hywel and Cadwallon Crek, the descendants of Cadwallon ap Madog, came to the king at Worcester to do homage. Radnor itself had passed into the guardianship of Ralph Mortimer as early as 1235 and although the Tosnys had regained Painscastle by 1238, Ralph Tosny died young and early in 1241 his lands were granted to Queen Eleanor. Already it can be seen that Radnorshire was slipping from Dafydd's impotent hands. However, by this date Dafydd had decided upon the final arbitrator—war! On 14 June, King Henry wrote deploring Dafydd's actions in sending seneschalls to Henry's men of Ceri (the descendants of Cadwallon ap Madog) one of whom, Owain Fychan of Mechain, co-ordinated their attacks on Ralph Mortimer in Radnorshire. In spite of the promising start, the revolt in Maelienydd proved abortive and on 14 August Maredudd ap Maelgwn and his relations sought peace with the Crown and made a truce with Ralph Mortimer. This truce was to last until 29 September; their peace with the Crown remaining whether or not they went to war with Mortimer after the expiry of the truce! Just before 29 September the sorry Welsh lords of Maelienydd and Ceri again trekked to the king's court, this time no doubt to ensure their safety from the victorious lord of Wigmore. On 29 August, 1241, Ralph Mortimer had confirmed his victory by having the descendants of the Lords of Gwrtheyrnion quitclaim their lands to him as their natural lord. A few days later Llywelyn ap Gruffydd, the future Prince of Wales, renounced all his rights to Gwrtheyrnion and Maelienydd and promised to aid Ralph Mortimer and his heirs in their holding of those lands. This treaty augured badly for the future, though neither party could have realised what was in store for them.

In the aftermath of the war Ralph Mortimer began building a series of new castles in Maelienydd, castles that were planned to guarantee his families' safe holding of these lands down through the subsequent generations. Little did he know how soon he would be grateful for them. In June, 1244, Dafydd once more broke out in furious revolt and Ralph Mortimer and Humphrey Bohun were hard pressed to hold on to Brycheiniog and Radnorshire. The Welsh lords of Maelienydd and Ceri threw their might behind the rebellion, but in Elfael the descendants of Einion Clud held to their royal fealty. Then in January, 1245, the rebel army was smashed by royal forces near Montgomery and the threat to Radnorshire was lifted as suddenly as it had appeared, although on 26 October, Humphrey Bohun and Ralph Mortimer were still campaigning in the Marches between Shrewsbury and Brecon. Even after this, Dafydd was not crushed and he continued fighting from his Snowdonia fastnesses until death overtook him in February, 1246. Llywelyn ap Gruffydd and his elder brother Owain Goch succeeded him. His victory in Radnorshire beyond doubt, Ralph Mortimer died soon after Dafydd and on 10 August his brother Philip and widow Gwladys Ddu were ordered to surrender Cefnllys and Knucklas castles to the king's officials.

On 26 February, 1247, the young Roger Mortimer, born in 1231, paid 2,000 marks to hold his father's lands. He also held claim to southern Radnorshire as the heir of William Braose through the right of his wife Matilda Braose. However, despite the young Roger's claims Painscastle was returned to Petronilla the widow of Ralph Tosny on 23 November, 1247. This left just Elfael Uwch Mynydd in native control under the descendants of Einion Clud and under the acquisitive eye of Roger Mortimer. The following ten years were a time of peace, and in that peace there was plenty of time for contemplation and for old grudges to rancour. Under the direction of the king everything was given over to compromise, but what the king lacked was authority to enforce his sensible decisions. Thus the division of the Braose inheritance led to a smouldering resentment on the part of Roger Mortimer who felt (quite rightly) that he was not given a third part of the lands that were his entitlement. Consequently it is of little surprise that Roger attempted to gain all that land he felt entitled to when the final arbitrator was once again war.

In the meantime peace and litigation were the order of the day in Radnorshire. In 1248, Roger Vaughan, the son and heir of Gwallter Clud, with the powerful backing of Petronilla Tosny, claimed Elfael Uwch Mynydd from Owain ap Maredudd ab Einion Clud, who was holding the land as tenant in chief of the Crown. On this occasion Roger lost, though later his son Rhys would rise to prominence in the land. In the spring of 1249 two of the dispossessed descendants of Cadwallon ap Madog, Maredudd ap Maelgwn and Hywel ap Cadwallon, wended their way to the king from Gwynedd where they had been living in a pitiful state, begging restitution of at least some part of their once great patrimony. The men of the Marches in horror reported to the king that these were the first men to throw off their allegiance to the Crown in previous wars as had their fathers and grandfathers before them; they were traitors and felons and deserved to suffer the fate of their ancestors, righteously hanged by good King John at Bridgnorth in 1212 'for felony as seditious persons and enemies'! With this damming judgment Maredudd ap Maelgwn, who under the auspices of Llywelyn ab Iorwerth had ruled Maelienydd for 25 successful years, returned to the wildernesses he had inhabited since the death of Dafydd. Cadwallon, his nephew, also disappeared from the scene for many long years. After a brief imprisonment in Caus Castle in 1253 for killing his cousin, he is next found with Maredudd's son, Llywelyn, in Prince Llywelyn's service meeting the king's representatives at the ford of Montgomery in 1260. In southern Elfael, 1251 saw Roger Tosny partially regaining Painscastle in his mother's name, following Welsh practice. The same year he and the earl of Hereford, who was the royal constable of the castle, were ordered to restore Godfrey Gamages to his lands in Boughrood and Trewern, which may have been in the king's hands as part of Elfael Is Mynydd since the reconquest of Llywelyn's lands from Prince Dafydd in 1240/1.

In 1252, Gwilym ap Gwrwared, the royal constable of Genau'r Glyn and Iscoed, by the command of the king, carried off great spoil from the men of Elenydd because they claimed the pastures of Maelienydd by right. This was the only sign of impending destruction for many of the castles of Radnorshire on an as yet relatively untroubled horizon. The same year, on 20 November, Roger Mortimer of Wigmore fought and lost a legal battle that sought to establish that Radnor was in the Marches of Wales and the resultant loss of his Marcher liberties of private justice would have been a great financial and humiliating blow. The year before Walter Clifford had come within an ace of outright war against the king over his liberty of Clifford. With Wales peaceful the king could ride roughshod over the jealously guarded liberties of the Marches, but for his illegality the king would later be repaid by the legitimate grievances carefully nurtured by his betrayed baronage.

In 1254, Henry III decided to settle large estates upon his eldest son, Prince Edward, as heir apparent. At a stroke all the king's lands in Wales were suddenly in the hands of the prince. According to the charter which Henry drew up, this included the whole county of Chester with its castles and towns and with the king's conquest of Wales in these bounds, Rhuddlan, Dysserth and Degannwy with the other lands of the Perfeddwlad, Bristol, the Trilateral, Montgomery, Carmarthen, Cardigan and Buellt. Not mentioned, but obviously granted, probably as a subsidiary of the nearby lordship of Buellt, were the lands of Sir Owain ap Maredudd in Elfael Uwch Mynydd. Edward's new administrators of the Welsh were men like Alan la Zouche, a relation of Roger Mortimer, and Geoffrey Langley—men who openly boasted of their intention to tax the Welsh until their pips squeaked! In the Middle Ages such a policy could only mean one of two things—absolute surrender and possible starvation, or total resistance. It is to their credit that the Welsh of Edward's principality endured four long years of resentment and ill treatment before recourse to an inevitable war was taken. The catalyst for the war itself seems to have been Edward when, in the autumn of 1256, he visited his Welsh domains. The native population, who refused to believe that their prince would countenance the injustice being done to them in his name, discovered to their horror that Edward in his youthful impecuniosity was firmly of the opinion that his underlings were serving him well. In shock the tenants of the Perfeddwlad called in Llywelyn ap Gruffydd to save them from this unbearable oppression. On 1 November, 1256, to the cheers of the oppressed Welsh and with the goodwill of the less, but equally oppressed Marchers, Llywelyn and Dafydd ap Gruffydd crossed the border.

The Rule of Llywelyn ap Gruffydd 1256–77
Llywelyn's invasion of the Perfeddwlad could have had little initial effect on Roger Mortimer, who may well have been one of the Marcher Lords said to have regarded Llywelyn's enterprise with

understanding, if not active support. However, as Llywelyn swept south annexing Meirionydd, Ceredigion and Buellt Roger's suspicions may have been aroused and he became incensed when Llywelyn seized Gwrtheyrnion against the treaty he and Ralph Mortimer had made in 1241. Llywelyn had made an enemy who would eventually bring about his ruin and death. In Radnorshire the scene was set for the opening rounds of 'the great Welsh war', as the citizens of Shrewsbury were to refer to it after its conclusion twenty years later.

On 15 October, 1256, Roger Tosny was finally adjudged of age and allowed to assume full responsibility for his lands at Painscastle and he immediately began legal proceedings against Henry Pembridge who held the Elfael manors and castles of Boughrood and Trewern from the Crown in right of his wife, Elizabeth Gamages. To the north, possibly at Aberedw, lay the lands of Owain ab Iorwerth Clud. He died the same year and was apparently succeeded by his cousin Sir Owain Fychan ap Maredudd and his children, who held Aberedw until the revolt of 1282. Owain ap Maredudd also held the entire land of Elfael Uwch Mynydd which was bounded to the north by the barony of Radnor, now held by Roger Mortimer in right of his Braose wife. Maelienydd to the west was held by the right of the conquest of Ralph Mortimer way back in the eleventh century, though as we have seen Mortimer rule there rarely exceeded 20 years duration at any one time. In the far west of Radnorshire lay Gwrtheyrnion and Elenydd, conquered by Roger Mortimer, perhaps for the first time just before 1200 and held, except for the interruption by Llywelyn, by the Mortimers and their vassals. Virtually surrounded by the Mortimer fiefs lay another little Marcher lordship, that of Bleddfa. This fee, probably carved out by Richard fitz Scope in the eleventh century, had descended to the Mortimers of Norfolk, followers of the Earls of Warenne, who had supplanted the Mortimers of Wigmore in their Norman home vill in 1054. This was the state of Radnorshire at the commencement of the twenty year's war.

From first to last the bulk of the war in Radnorshire fell on the shoulders of one man. On 18 January, 1257, Roger Mortimer was granted protection 'so long as he was engaged on the king's business in Wales'. Within days the royal records speak of the army of

Roger Mortimer and there can be no doubt that Roger was intending to regain Gwrtheyrnion seized by his treacherous cousin, Llywelyn. Late that summer two royal armies joined Roger in Wales, but there was no success for any English venture that year. From now on Roger's main support in, as the king described it, 'his' (Roger's) war against the Welsh, was promises of money from the Exchequer; promises that were never realised! The young Prince Edward, later to be known as 'The Hammer of the Scots', probably did far more to alleviate Roger's problems than the king when he granted him his royal rights in Elfael Uwch Mynydd and the allegiance of the princelings there—Owain ap Maredudd and Owain ab Iorwerth Clud. This may have been little more than the recognition of King John's grant of 1200 to William Braose, but for Mortimer it was a sign of encouragement even if the immediate future looked particularly bleak.

It was around this time that Henry Pembridge came to the forefront of affairs in southern Elfael. He was sheriff of Hereford and lord of Boughrood in right of his wife, Elizabeth Gamages, and from 1257 onwards was leading the king's Monmouth based army against the Welsh.

Such was the situation in Radnorshire when the great constitutional crisis swept over the whole land, and the baronage of England united to save Henry III from his pecuniary disasters and to 'reform the state of England'. The resultant 'Mad Parliament of Oxford' did nothing to aid Roger Mortimer in his struggle against the Welsh, but did lead to him being appointed one of the barons' representatives on the King's Council. This political revolution had many far reaching consequences, one of which was the disgrace and exile of the Earl of Pembroke who accused the reformers of treason in regard to the prosecution of the now officially abandoned Welsh campaign. As many of the leaders of the reformation were Marcher lords—Mortimer, Bohun, Pembridge, Gloucester—and were themselves being damaged through the Welsh truce, the charge can probably be seen as insincere. In the ensuing confusion Roger Tosny of Painscastle decided to try to reclaim his ancient inheritance in northern Elfael and began to encroach on the territories of both Mortimer and Pembridge, causing the two outraged Marchers to appeal to the Crown on 22 June, 1258.

It was a brittle Welsh truce agreed at the Mad Parliament which lasted through the next two years. On 23 April, 1260, the Welsh of Ceri, undoubtedly led by Llywelyn ap Maredudd and Hywel ap Cadwallon, with their allies of Cedewain, poured down the Teme valley and sacked the undefended town of Knighton. As a consequence, on 8 May, the king granted Roger Mortimer the right to raise taxes to build a wall around the town for its protection. However, the most frequent interruptions were caused by Llywelyn and his supporters in Deheubarth invading Buellt and attacking the castle at Builth Wells. Several times Roger Mortimer, who had eventually been entrusted with the defence of the castle and cantref, had to rush west to break the siege and force Llywelyn's forces back. In this he was aided by Owain ap Maredudd of Elfael, whose own son Madog was amongst the castle's defenders when it was subsequently treacherously surrendered to Llywelyn's besiegers on 17 July, 1260. As a consequence of Madog's capture Owain was forced to do homage to Llywelyn and pay him 300 marks for his son's release. As a result of the capitulation of the fortress Llywelyn was excommunicated for violating the sworn truce whilst a major campaign was called for against him. However, all that happened was that Roger and other Marcher lords were ordered to go to Llywelyn and arrange yet another truce, which they successfully did in the August of 1260. The fall of Elfael Uwch Mynydd to Llywelyn was a serious blow to the prestige of Roger Mortimer and over the next four years his situation worsened as the rest of Radnorshire fell to Llywelyn's burgeoning power.

The Prince of Gwynedd could afford to be generous with truces as he stood quietly aside and watched the government of England steadily rend itself apart. In December, 1261, the king formally pardoned those barons who had acted against him in the reformation of the state, the deeds of Roger Mortimer being especially mentioned and forgiven. Early the next year the king wrote to Llywelyn saying how glad he was that the prince was not espousing the cause of the Reformers and was staying isolated from English politics. However, as soon as he heard that Llywelyn was seriously ill he prepared for the invasion of Wales! Such duplicitous plans proved abortive, but confirmed Llywelyn in his obstinacy. In November, 1262, his friends struck the blow which Llywelyn must have been deliberating. Probably a little before 27 November the Welsh of Maelienydd, allegedly on their own initiative, decided to wrest Radnorshire from Roger Mortimer. Consequently they stormed Cefnllys Castle by night and called Llywelyn's officials to them. They rapidly came to the place, perhaps having been fore-warned, and destroyed the castle. The same day Bleddfa Castle was overwhelmed and destroyed for the last time. The aged Brian Brampton of Brampton Bryan, already at least 60 years old and with another 10 years of campaigning and crusading before him, sensing what was to come, made his will on 27 November and marched out for Cefnllys at the side of his lord, Roger Mortimer.

At Cefnllys the Marcher army came face to face with disaster, for Llywelyn had come south with his entire host. The startled captains of the March calculated that Llywelyn had with him some 300 heavy cavalry and 30,000 foot. Against them stood only Roger Mortimer and Humphrey Bohun Junior with their hastily raised Marcher troops, the flower of the young men of the Marches. The action proved short and sharp and the Marcher forces were rapidly bottled up in the ruined and unprovisioned walls of Cefnllys Castle. Llywelyn did not wait to reduce the defiant troops, but, surrounding Cefnllys, he pushed on with part of his army taking the homage of Roger's vassals of Radnorshire and attacking Roger's castles with his siege train. On 24 December, 1262, the king, landing at Dover on his return from France, learnt of Roger's plight and immediately began to organise for his relief, something which the government of England had omitted to do. However, by 28 December, the war for northern Radnorshire was over. Roger's castles of Knucklas, Presteign, Knighton and Norton had surrendered to Llywelyn 'through fear of his siege engines'. Without hope of succour Roger accepted his cousin Llywelyn's offer of a free passage through his lines back to England. Without food or hope of relief the dreadfully thinned ranks of the Marcher army tramped its frozen path back to Wigmore Castle, amongst hypocritical cries of treason from an impotent government that had abandoned Roger and Humphrey's armies to their fate. At Wigmore in his 'compulsive and vehement anger' Roger plotted his vengeance against all concerned.

With Roger's defeat the Welsh of Painscastle revoked their alle-giance to the king and did homage to Llywelyn as too did the

The Campaign of 1262

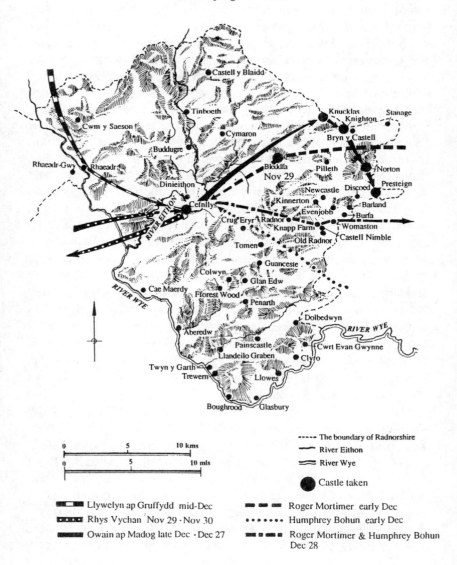

Castell y Blaidd
Tinboeth
Cwm y Saeson
Cymaron
Knucklas
Knighton
Stanage
Bryn y Castell
Buddugre
Blodfa
Nov 29
Pilleth
Norton
Rhaeadr-Gwy
Rhaeadr
Discoed
Presteign
Dinieithon
Newcastle
Barland
Cefnllys
Kinnerton
Evenjobb
Burfa
Crug Eryr
Radnor
Knapp Farm
Womaston
Old Radnor
Castell Nimble
Tomen
Guanceste
Colwyn
Glan Edw
Cae Maerdy
Fforest Wood
Penarth
Dolbedwyn
RIVER WYE
Aberedw
Cwrt Evan Gwynne
Painscastle
Clyro
Twyn y Garth
Llandeilo Graben
Trewern
Llowes
Boughrood
Glasbury

RIVER EITHON
RIVER WYE

0   5   10 kms
0   5   10 mls

- - - - - The boundary of Radnorshire
———— River Eithon
≈≈≈≈ River Wye
● Castle taken

Llywelyn ap Gruffydd mid-Dec
Rhys Vychan Nov 29 · Nov 30
Owain ap Madog late Dec · Dec 27

Roger Mortimer early Dec
Humphrey Bohun early Dec
Roger Mortimer & Humphrey Bohun
Dec 28

49

Welsh of Brecon and Gwent. The Norman gains of 200 years had been lost at a stroke. In early January, 1263, the king recalled Prince Edward from Gascony. Meantime Roger Mortimer regrouped his forces at Wigmore and then struck out with determination at his ever multiplying enemies, knowing well that the longer the battle was put off the better prepared those enemies would be. On 1 February, 1263, Humphrey Bohun Senior, the inactive commander of royal forces in the Marches, was replaced by John Grey who set up his headquarters at Abergavenny. On 2 February, Roger Mortimer's new army was blessed at Wigmore Abbey and a few days later joined with royal forces at Ludlow where they received the king's writ declaring that the army was composed of his men on his business for the coming campaign. Mortimer with his massed army, Grey with only 12 knights, Humphrey Bohun Senior, Reginald fitz Peter of Blaenllyfni and some mounted sergeants and footmen moved westwards, joining their forces at Brecon where they were met by Llywelyn's troops, reckoned at 180 cavalry and 10,000 foot. No battle took place and after a day or two the Marchers moved southwards to Abergavenny which was sorely pressured by another Welsh force under the princes of Deheubarth. Just north of Abergavenny, on 3 March, the combined Marcher armies routed the Welsh skirmishers and sent the main host fleeing over Blorenge mountain, leaving between 300 and 500 of their number slain or captured. Although the battles of Cefnllys and Abergavenny had not been full pitched battles, as had Painscastle the previous century, they proved just as decisive. Welsh advance in the Marches had been crowned by Cefnllys but was stopped at Abergavenny.

The question now was whether Roger Mortimer and the Marcher coalition was strong enough to throw Llywelyn out of Radnorshire. The time looked favourable for Prince Edward now appeared on the scene with his Flemish mercenaries and campaigned with Mortimer as far as Brecon, where Llywelyn's new castle at Sennybridge was attacked and destroyed and all Brycheiniog was transferred to Roger Mortimer as the heir of William Braose, to the chagrin of the Bohun Earls of Hereford. However, an advance into Radnorshire was not made and Edward withdrew much of the Marcher army northwards to Chester. In the meantime Roger Mortimer based himself at Radnor Castle and at the end of March continued his war until, around 25 April, he was seriously wounded by a Welsh arrow. With the temporary loss of their lord, Brecon Castle shamefully surrendered to Llywelyn. At this point the war with Llywelyn took on a national outlook as England itself dissolved into civil war due, according to one chronicler, to the arrogance of Prince Edward and Roger Mortimer. The civil war proved disastrous to the attempt to regain Radnorshire, for most of the Marchers except Mortimer supported Simon de Montfort and the reformers against King Henry and Prince Edward. Llywelyn was allowed to secure and expand his gains, with most Marchers temporarily accepting the loss of their Welsh lands in the interests of victory against royal policy.

In early February, 1264, Llywelyn with his new ally Gruffydd ap Gwenwynwyn of Powys moved south to eliminate the last Mortimer stronghold in Radnorshire, Radnor Castle itself. Throughout February the king ordered various royal officials to muster their forces for Roger's aid, but it can be imagined that little was done by Marcher lords who had already arrayed themselves against the royalist cause. On about 15 March, Radnor Castle succumbed and all Radnorshire was in the hands of Llywelyn. To cap his success, Painscastle, if it had not already done so, surrendered to the prince and was destroyed. Llywelyn now held Radnorshire far more powerfully than Rhys ap Gruffydd had done nearly a century before. However, Llywelyn's victory was not without consequence, for the Marchers, angered by the impotence of the government to protect their lands, began to turn to Prince Edward and Roger Mortimer for succour. The birth of a new movement in the Marches had occurred, but it was not to see fruition until 4 August, 1265, when they helped destroy Simon de Montfort at the battle of Evesham and reinstate royal rule. Now at last they could return to deal with Llywelyn who was occupying their ancestral lands.

Immediately before the battle of Evesham one of the most crucial treaties of Anglo–Welsh history was struck just outside Radnorshire. On 19 June, 1265, at Pipton Castle on the River Wye, Prince Llywelyn made a great treaty with Simon de Montfort and Henry III who at the time were corresponding with him from Hereford, where they were being harassed by Prince Edward and

Roger Mortimer. This treaty made on the very boundaries of Llywelyn's principality at the edge of Radnorshire granted Llywelyn his life's ambition—the full recognition by the Crown of his title of Prince of Wales and of his conquests throughout Wales and in Radnorshire. Llywelyn was triumphant.

Although Henry III repudiated the treaty of Pipton after he was rescued at Evesham, the continuation of the war by Roger Mortimer and others could not reverse the outcome and at Montgomery on 29 September, 1267, another treaty was drawn up, little different in extent to that which was granted to Llywelyn in 1265. Llywelyn kept the lordship of Painscastle, until Ralph Tosny should be of age, and kept the homage of the men of Maelienydd in northern Radnorshire, at least until Roger Mortimer had rebuilt his castle at Cefnllys, when justice should be done concerning the contending claims of Roger and Llywelyn. Such justice was never carried out and by default Roger appears to have been allowed by Llywelyn to recover seisin. As late as 1273 Llywelyn was complaining of Roger's conduct, but he did nothing to disturb the peace. Instead he awaited the onslaught that must certainly come from his refusal to do homage to Edward I (1272-1307) or his representatives.

On his return from Crusade in 1274, King Edward moved slowly and patiently with his cousin of Gwynedd. Such deliberation, however, could only benefit Edward as Llywelyn's vassals one by one began to fall away from him, merely by the implicit threat of violence that would befall opponents of royal power. First to show signs of wavering were the princelings of Elfael who in May, 1276, found it necessary to make a series of charters guaranteeing their faith to Llywelyn and ransoming those whose faith was not quite so secure! Before 24 June, 1276, Roger Mortimer and his allies began the long awaited campaign against the Welsh of Central Wales, attacking their lands 'with a great multitude of horse and foot, with flags flying'. Then, just before 15 July, Roger seized 122 merchants of Wales at Leominster and Montgomery, which included men from Elfael and Gwrtheyrnion. Llywelyn's bailiff of these districts, Rhys ap Gruffydd, complained bitterly, but impotently to Llywelyn. The seizure of such merchants was a sure sign of war as they would probably have been stocking up for the purposes of war and in war it was common to deny your enemies all sustenance.

On 16 November, Roger Mortimer was appointed captain of Shropshire, Staffordshire and Herefordshire against Llywelyn ap Gruffydd and his allies—the war had royal sanction. The following day Ralph Tosny was told to receive the Welsh of Elfael Is Mynydd, adherents of Llywelyn ap Gruffydd, into the king's peace and on the next day he was granted a safe conduct in going to the Marches on the king's affairs. Roger Mortimer, on hearing of this, again claimed that King John had given to Matilda his wife the land of Elfael Is Mynydd and seized Painscastle. He only relinquished it to the king under protest on 26 January, 1277, when a local inquisition found against him and his claim.

Because of the campaign's winter start Roger Mortimer complained that he could not get supplies of wine from Bristol for stocking his castles nor provisions for men arriving in the March. He was further worried that iron, salt, and food were reaching his enemies in Wales from Scotland, Norway and the Isle of Man; Roger certainly had no qualms that this war was of the utmost seriousness. As the weather improved so the campaigning began in earnest and by the end of the spring Gwrtheyrnion again fell to the forces of Mortimer, though Roger himself was probably campaigning to the north at the time, helping pen Llywelyn up in his highland fastness of Snowdonia. By 16 August, 1277, Roger Mortimer and Humphrey Bohun had a force of 2,700 men from the Middle Marches of Buellt, Brecon, Elfael, Maelienydd and Gwrtheyrnion active for the king[1]. Radnorshire was finally reconquered for the Crown, largely by the forces of, and under the auspice of the most formidable and single-minded of the Marcher Lords, Roger Mortimer of Wigmore.

---

1. The force was led by Hywel ap Meurig, whilst the various contingents from Radnorshire consisted of, from Roger Mortimer's land of Elfael Uwch Mynydd, Ifor ap Gruffydd the bailiff of Colwyn; from Maelienydd and Elfael came a further 109 foot under Llywelyn ap Philip, Maredudd ap Hywel, Adam Goch, Hywel ap Madog and Cadwgan ap Maredudd; from Radnor came 300 foot and horse under Meurig ab Ithel; from Elfael (Is Mynydd?) came 240 foot under Ifor ap Gruffydd and finally from Colwyn came 400 foot under Iordan ap Maredudd and Madog ap Llywelyn.

Revolts and Marcher Rule 1278–1400

With the conquest of the Welsh Marches in 1276–77 peace once again came to the disputed border of England and Wales, although now and again the serenity would be shattered by violent outbursts. The first such outbreak involved Llywelyn ap Gruffydd.

After the resumption of Mortimer rule in northern Elfael, Maelienydd and Gwrtheyrnion, litigation was the order of the day. Various Welsh vassals made claims against Roger Mortimer and the Mortimers made claims against their neighbours. On 22 July, 1278, Elizabeth Pembridge, the widow of Henry, claimed Boughrood and Trewern with their castles from Rhys ap Roger who had been granted them during the occupation of Prince Llywelyn. Rhys was, not surprisingly, ordered to be ejected from his manors, thus eliminating the last descendant of Gwallter Clud from lands in Radnorshire. However, Rhys was not prepared to let the matter rest and the following year brought the case again to the Hopton Commission which was adjudicating the legal situation in the Marches. Again he failed in his plea. In 1281, Ifor ap Gruffydd found himself having to legally defend his lands in Elfael against John Braose, who claimed them as the descendant of the William Braose Junior who had been starved to death by King John in 1210. In these litigations the local Welsh almost invariably found themselves at a disadvantage, and that disadvantage inevitably led to dissatisfaction.

On 9 October, 1281, Llywelyn ap Gruffydd came to Radnor for the last time. Here he met his cousin and adversary of old, Roger Mortimer, and together they signed a pact of friendship against all men—except for the king! What were they planning? The quitclaim by Llywelyn of certain lands to Roger seems to indicate that their common enemy was Gruffydd ap Gwenwynwyn and his son Owain, against whom both were now pursuing lengthy court cases. Events had now come full circle. The Prince of Wales had come to enlist the support of the man who for twenty years had been his main adversary in the Marches. It has been suggested that as Llywelyn had married late and as yet had no heir, although his wife was pregnant, Roger, as a grandson of Llywelyn the Great, was aiming to succeed Llywelyn as Prince of Wales to the exclusion of Llywelyn's despised and largely ineffectual brothers, Dafydd,

Rhodri and Owain Goch. Whatever the intention of these Radnor talks, one fact was certain, both men were playing for high stakes, and Llywelyn himself was already set on war! Throughout the previous four long years Llywelyn had had humiliation after humiliation poured upon him by the English administration of the conquered lands of Wales. However, it was not just Llywelyn who felt aggrieved, nearly all who lived in Wales had their grievances; grievances that were inevitable with so many claims and counter-claims to hand. All it needed was one spark to light the old embers of discontent. Llywelyn, with the help of his dark and hot-headed brother Dafydd, lit that spark.

Throughout the winter of 1281–82 Llywelyn built up his supplies, his merchants acquiring as much lead, a valuable war material, as they could. On 2 February, 1282, Llywelyn, at his wife's labour and eventual death bed in Llyn, wrote to Edward a last despairing letter listing his grievances. Looked at with hindsight it was a certain precursor of war. On the night of 21 March, 1282, Dafydd attacked and once more Wales was alight the length and breadth of the country, though the lands under the sway of Roger Mortimer stayed strangely aloof. War occurred in Gwynedd, Powys and Deheubarth, but in Radnorshire nothing is recorded as stirring. Perhaps an agreement had been made with Roger Mortimer.

On 25 March, the king placed Roger in charge of the Middle March and made all the Marchers dependent upon him. In the meantime Dafydd ripped south through Powys and stormed the ancestral English-held castles of the Princes of Deheubarth with the aid of their dispossessed descendants. Throughout the long summer Roger Mortimer campaigned in eastern Powys bringing Overton, Bromfield, Montgomery and Chirk firmly under royal control. On 2 September, £500 was sent from the king who was then at Chester to Roger Mortimer 'to expedite certain special business of the king in those parts where up to the present ... [text destroyed] ... And if ... he needs ... to take the said money to his lord, then the escort which he ...'. The document was sealed with the king's private seal. What did this mean? Was there really a plot afoot between Roger and Llywelyn and was it expedited with the king's contrivance? That we shall probably never know. But what did happen next threw

The Campaign of 1282

Llywelyn ap Gruffydd

Castell y Blaidd

Tinboeth

Knucklas
Knighton
Stanage

Cwm y Saeson

Cymaron

Bryn y Castell

Abbey Cwmhir
Dec 10

Buddugre

Rhaeadr-Gwy   Rhaeadr

Bleddfa
Pilleth
Norton

Dinieithon

Presteign

Cefnllys

Newcastle
Discoed

Barland

Kinnerton

RIVER EITHON

Crug Eryr
Radnor
Evenjobb
Burfa

Knapp Farm
Womaston

Old Radnor
Castell Nimble

Tomen

Guanceste

Colwyn
Glan Edw

Cae Maerdy

RIVER WYE

Fforest Wood
Penarth

Builth

Dolbedwyn

Dec 11

Aberedw

RIVER WYE

Painscastle
Cwrt Evan Gwynne

Llandeilo Graben
Clyro

Twyn y Garth

Trewern
Llowes

Boughrood   Glasbury

0 ———— 5 ———— 10 kms

0 ———— 5 ———— 10 mls

----- The boundary of Radnorshire
——— River Eithon
═══ River Wye

56

Radnorshire into turmoil and certainly suggests that Roger was this time favouring the Welsh in the war. On 15 October, Roger's bailiffs of Knighton, Radnor and either Clun or Colwyn were ordered by the government to cease supplying Llywelyn's needs! This does not seem to be the actions of the Roger Mortimer of old. Whatever was intended, an unexpected twist now threw any plot out of joint, for on 16 October, Roger suddenly died at Kingsland in Herefordshire, aged 51. The war with Llywelyn now took its final turn.

The prince, hearing of Roger's death and in possession of a document which seemed, using false names, to indicate that many in the Marches were willing to follow him, moved southwards with the intention of raising Radnorshire and the surrounding districts to his cause. It was to be his penultimate mistake. On Roger's death, Roger Springhose, the sheriff of Shropshire, was granted custody of the Mortimer lands and he rapidly made a tour of inspection of the castles and ensured that the garrisons were paid. At first he was satisfied with the situation and two years later reported to the Exchequer that he had spent the following sums on garrisons in the Mortimer castles; at New Radnor 4 horse and 12 foot for £8 2s.; at Cefnllys 8 horse and 20 foot for £15 10s. 6d.; at Tinboeth 5 horse and 30 foot for £13 16s. 9d.; and finally at Knucklas 8 horse and 20 foot for £15 10s. 6d. It is interesting to note the differences in the garrisons, but we can only wonder at the reasons for these variations in size and composition. In November, the sheriff began to pick up strange undercurrents from Roger's tenants and wrote in alarm to the king that he 'had negotiated the inhabitants into the king's peace so far as he was able, in accordance with the king's instructions. But he had found the inhabitants very fickle and haughty as though they were on the point of leaving the king's peace, because they had no definite lord; and he believed that they would not long remain in peace if their liege lord did not come to them'. The king rapidly reacted to the warning and on 24 November, Edmund Mortimer was made responsible for his father's lands. In this respect the king acted judiciously, for the last act in the life of Prince Llywelyn was about to be played out.

On 10 December, 1282, Llywelyn marched into Radnorshire, entering the Wye Valley from the Berwyn mountains where he had been opposing Roger Lestrange. The prince marched on Rhayader with 160 cavalry and 7,000 foot and took the homage of the men there without resistance. That night he stayed in nearby Abbey Cwmhir, where his grandfather had lavished so much money on the impressive church set in the isolated mountain valley of Maelienydd. While he was there all the potentates of the March— Roger Lestrange, John Giffard, the sons of Roger Mortimer— Edmund, Roger, William and Geoffrey, Robert Mortimer of Richard's Castle and Bleddfa, together with Gruffydd ap Gwenwynwyn of Powys—gathered their forces against him. The next day Llywelyn moved south, leaving Radnorshire, and entering the cantref of Buellt where he took the homage of the people as far as Llanganten, the original Builth Wells. Just west of the town, at Orwin Bridge, he left his army and with a small escort of 17 or 18 men he sped eastwards to keep a rendezvous, probably with the descendants of Einion Clud in nearby Elfael, whose borders almost bounded the castle of Builth itself. Certainly, after Llywelyn's death, Owain Fychan and his sons, Gruffydd, Madog and Iorwerth, were dispossessed of their lands for rebellion. Now was certainly their chance to rebel. However, even as these sturdy independents raised their flag of revolt, their time had passed. In confused circumstances, Llywelyn's bodyguard was intercepted and Llywelyn wounded and then beheaded. 3,000 of his army were then slaughtered for, according to the account of Roger Lestrange, the cost of no English casualties. Roger then had the prince's severed head sent to King Edward at Rhuddlan with a hasty account of the action. Archbishop Peckham, who was nearby, came to the scene and removed a 'certain schedule, expressed in obscure words and fictitious names, a copy of which Edmund Mortimer has, which was found in the breeches of Llywelyn, formerly Prince of Wales, together with his small seal, which the archbishop is causing to be kept safely for the king. From this schedule the bishop can sufficiently guess that certain magnates, neighbours of the Welsh, either Marchers or others, are not too loyal to the king, wherefore let the king be warned unless he come to some damage'. This is the last that was ever heard of the schedule.

In the north, Llywelyn's death was met with dismay and the revolt rapidly collapsed, although his brother, Dafydd, kept fighting until the bitter end, unsuccessfully sending John ap Dafydd of Arwystli to Radnorshire to try and keep the standards flying in late May, 1283. But the end of the war had come and most, including the much lamenting bards, knew it. In Radnorshire, Mortimer was triumphant, only in southern Elfael was there any opposition to their rule and this came from the house of Tosny which had long been dispossessed of various lands. For the next 40 years indeterminable court cases rumbled on concerning the conflicting claims to Aberedw, Boughrood, Glasbury, Painscastle and Colwyn, which the Beauchamps, as heirs to the Tosnys, eventually won, mainly through Mortimer indifference as they by then held far more profitable lands than the mountains of Elfael.

The next Welsh revolt began in June, 1287, when Rhys ap Maredudd, oppressed by the local officials and unable to achieve judicial recompense, went to war. To meet this threat Edmund Mortimer reluctantly formed an army from his Marcher lands and marched against Dryslwyn Castle some time after 15 August. The revolt was unsuccessful and despite government worries did not spread to Radnorshire or elsewhere in Wales. During the peace that followed we have a description of the main settlements of Radnorshire listed as being in the diocese of St Davids; Radnor was not included as it had been incorporated into the diocese of Hereford, probably by the king or his Braose successor to the land, and most likely in the eleventh century. Thus Edmund Mortimer could claim around that time that Elfael consisted of three constituent parts, Is Mynydd, Uwch Mynydd and Aberedw, ignoring Radnor, which had been a constituent part of old[1]. From the 1291 taxation list it can be seen that the main population centres have changed little in the past eight hundred and probably thousand years.

The year 1294 saw war once again. Cefnllys Castle succumbed to the men of Maelienydd who rose in the general rising of Madog

---

1. The churches in the 1291 taxation list included in Elfael: Glascwm, Disserth, Llansanffraid, Aberedw, Gladestry, Bryngwyn, Clyro, Llowes, Llanbedr Painscastle, Llandegelli which may have been Llanfihangel Llechryd, Cregrina, Llanelwedd and Boughrood. In the deaconry of Maelienydd there were churches at Llanbister, Nantmel, Ceri, Buddugre, Langmilles/Langmiclen, Llanfihangel Nant Melan, St Germans, Lanemeth, Lanpadarn, Llandegley, Llanddewi/Llanbister, Bleddfa and Rhayader.

ap Llywelyn of Meirionydd, Cynan ap Maredudd of Deheubarth and Morgan ap Maredudd of Gwynllwg. On 8 March, 1295, Edmund Mortimer was given permission to bring his Welsh back into the royal fealty (as they had rebelled against the Crown), especially those of Gwrtheyrnion and Ceri. Even with this royal sanction Edmund Mortimer found it wise to make many concessions to his men of Radnorshire, indicating the current situation in the Marches. Just before 1 June, 1297, Edmund granted his men of Maelienydd the right to be heard at his court of Cymaron by the common law of England on condition that they never again raised any action against him concerning his demesne of Cefnllys, Knucklas or Pilleth. Also mentioned were the hundreds of Knucklas and Cefnllys apparently as they had existed in Roger Mortimer's time in the 1270s. Radnorshire had clearly been divided into hundreds with courts at Cefnllys, Knucklas, Cymaron, and Colwyn (Hundred House), whilst we can almost certainly add to that list Rhayader, Radnor, Aberedw and Painscastle. It is apparent that the county was divided then much as it is today. The men of Maelienydd also paid £500 to have their hunting rights confirmed along the Eithon and in eastern Maelienydd.

When Edmund Mortimer died on 17 July, 1304, the Crown was strong enough for the first time to carry out an inquisition of the Mortimer lands in Wales. Inquisitions on the death of a noble were common in England from the twelfth century, but they were virtually unheard of in the Marches as the Marcher Lords claimed to hold their land by conquest and refused royal officials the right to examine their landholdings. Consequently, we gain a valuable insight into contemporary Radnorshire. In the manor of Radnor itself were the hamlets of Harpton, Downton, Walton, Cascob, Gladestry; the water mills of Ditch(mill), Crunkemere, Holbach and Radnor; rents from Old Radnor, Kinnerton, Saltford, Badland, Gliditon, Evenjobb; rents from the free tenants in Hymns Farm Chesewaldesleye, Sarnesfield (in Herefordshire), Bedelesput and 12 free tenants who rendered 6s. yearly for the upkeep of the castle, and finally several woods are mentioned called North Wood (east of Barland), Ack Wood (north of Ednol), Little Wood, Badland Wood and Radnor Wood. To the south the only vill in southern Radnor lordship was Gladestry, held for perhaps a century by the

Anglophile family of Hywel ap Meurig. To the north of Radnor the township of Presteign was held of Humphrey Bohun's lordship of Brecon for paying suit at his court of Huntington. In the rest of Radnorshire lay Knighton and Norton by Knighton in Welshry (a district populated by the Welsh), Pilleth in the Welshry of Wigmore, the commote of Gwrtheyrnion with the site of the ancient castle and town of Rhayader, of which 9 tenants rendered nothing because their lands were destroyed by war. Held of Radnor Lordship was the cantref of Maelienydd with Cefnllys Castle and town with 25 burgesses, together with water mills at Llandewi, Melynnok, Crug (Kruk Bechas), Whitton and Llanfihangel Rhydithon along with Tinboeth and Knucklas castles, Knucklas township and the court of Cymaron. To the south, Colwyn and Elfael Uwch Mynydd had been abandoned to the Tosnys of Painscastle after the death of Edmund's mother Maud. Thus it can be seen that Radnorshire was at this time quite prosperous, except for the war wasted land of Gwrtheyrnion.

Early in the fourteenth century Elfael passed to the Beauchamps of Worcestershire through Robert Tosny's eldest sister Alice who had inherited the land before 1309, thus ending the family's long and often fruitless association with the cantref. On 24 June, 1316, northern Radnorshire was mentioned again in a Mortimer indenture. Their lands consisted of Maelienydd with the castles of Cefnllys and Tinboeth and the land of Cwmwd Deuddwr, the castle and manor of Radnor, the land of Ceri with the castle of Knucklas, the manors of Knighton, Norton, Presteign and Pilleth, the manor and land of Gwrtheyrnion and the castle of Rhayader in the Marches of Wales, and which were all held in chief by Roger Mortimer on the death of Margaret, the widow of Edmund Mortimer, his mother. These were the Mortimer lands that in April and May, 1321, supplied the men that allowed Roger Mortimer to rise successfully against his Marcher enemies in Glamorgan and defy the king and his hated favourites who were blamed for the disastrous royal policy. However, they did not make Roger Mortimer and his uncle, another Roger, feel strong enough to oppose the feudal army of England, and on 13 January, 1322, they submitted to the king and had their lands forfeited and themselves imprisoned by a duplicitous King Edward II.

However, Roger Mortimer of Wigmore escaped from the Tower of London on 1 August, 1323, and fled to France. Once there he gathered support and invaded England with the Queen, Prince Edward and Earl Edmund of Kent in late September, 1326, with just 700 mercenary Hainaulters. They rapidly dispersed the king's disintegrating forces, Mortimer chasing the king and his shrinking retinue through Glamorgan, where on 16 November, Edward II was captured at Neath by Rhys of Bronllys, the son of Hywel of Meurig of Radnorshire, amongst others. For the next three years Roger Mortimer, once more possessed of northern Radnorshire, ruled England and Wales as regent and lover of Edward II's queen. The unfortunate and tyrannical Edward II met an unpleasant end at Mortimer's orders in the dungeon of Berkeley Castle in Gloucestershire.

According to an inquisition of 16 April, 1332, sometime in this period Madog Lloyd attacked Montgomery with the aid of the men of Ceri and Cedewain, Powys, Maelienydd and Gwrtheyrnion. This minor uprising, was just one of the many that punctuated the later part of the Middle Ages in Radnorshire, though the area was mainly at peace in the latter part of the fourteenth century. A singular survival of the court rolls from 1356 to 1360 from the hundreds of Buddugre, Dinieithon, Rhiwallt and the court of Cymaron have come down to us, showing a period of peace and tranquillity, punctuated not by war, but by the ever present outbreaks of Black Plague that interrupted the latter half of the century.

The Glyn Dwr Rebellion and the Civil War
The misery caused by the Black Death was nothing compared to that caused by the rising prosperity which helped lead to a final attempt to gain independence for Wales. As Richard II fled westwards to Wales for succour from his faithful Principality the stirrings of national revolt were already being felt. The crowning of the usurper Henry IV, who cared little for Welsh national pretensions and aspirations, was therefore a signal for revolt. Though the revolt at first proved slow-moving, once lit it burned for nigh on a generation. Early in the war, when Glyn Dwr was virtually an outlaw, he based himself in the Plynlimon region and from here moved into the Mortimer lands of Radnorshire almost at will. His interference

in the area was made easier by the minority of the young Roger Mortimer, his uncle Edmund being responsible for the land. In 1402, Glyn Dwr moved into the valley of the Lugg and Edmund advanced against him to Pilleth where, on the hill of Bryn Glas above the church, the two armies met. At first it looked as if the battle was going well for Edmund, but then his Welsh levies of Radnorshire changed sides and in a few minutes Edmund was wounded and captured, the surviving royalists of the Mortimer army retreating back down the Lugg in some haste. The king apparently accused Edmund of treachery and refused to have him ransomed, instead installing his own governors in Radnorshire and garrisoning the castles. Edmund in his anger at this real treachery sided with Glyn Dwr and married his eldest daughter, in the end preferring death by starvation at the siege of Harlech Castle in 1408, rather than surrender to his now hated king. The war in Radnorshire continued its bloody course, and although the rebels never took possession of the castles they did achieve the near total destruction of the countryside and economy.

The only actual siege that has been recorded in the county during the Glyn Dwr rebellion was one that never happened. According to an account by the Henriecian antiquarian Leland, Radnor Castle was taken by storm in 1401 and its garrison slaughtered. As Radnor Castle was amongst those of northern Radnorshire seized by the Crown on the fall of Mortimer at Pilleth, its destruction in 1401, before the Glyn Dwr revolt had really got underway, can therefore be seen as erroneous.

Regardless of fiction, the Welsh resurgence of 1402 had serious repercussions for the castles of Radnorshire and many of the derelict shells of once noble defensive structures were pushed rapidly into use. Aberedw and probably Colwyn had been abandoned by 1397 and were not considered to be of any further military use, but Cefnllys, Clyro, Painscastle and Radnor were all victualled and armed in 1403. The other castles of Radnorshire were never mentioned, at least in any military capacity, and it can be well imagined that they had succumbed to agricultural activity and money-saving during the previous peaceful and relatively prosperous period. However, by 1406, it was recorded that Cefnllys Castle and the lordships of Knighton and Knucklas (the castles were not mentioned) were 'so burned and wasted by the rebels that no profit could issue to the king without their better custody'. No castles seem to have been rebuilt as a result of this war and only Cefnllys was actually repaired in the 1430s though this too was a ruin by 1588.

Consequently, the military history of the county during the Civil War of 1642 to 1646 consisted merely of contending armies marching through Radnorshire in 1645, and the use of the manpower from the county to swell the king's ever depleting ranks. Only two sieges are recorded, those of Abbey Cwmhir in December, 1645, and of Radnor. That Cwmhir was used as a garrison by the royalists at the end of the war strongly suggests that no castles were seriously defensible in Radnorshire. It would seem likely that Radnor Castle had fallen to the Parliamentarians some little time before Cwmhir, though no account of the action has survived. In 1535 it had been recorded that only one tower of Radnor Castle was actually worth repairing and that tower was currently being used as the county prison. All that is actually known of the parliamentarian 'siege' is the few cannon balls found at the site during the early Victorian excavations, made for an abortive monument to the Duke of Wellington designed to dominate the vale of Radnor, just like the castle once did.

New Radnor

A large mound with at least one bailey and stretches of town walls
Location: At the top of the High Street in the town (SO 212 610)
Access: A path leads up the mound from near the road junction

This castle has a particularly chequered history. Probably begun in 1070 by Earl William fitz Osbern, it was captured in 1182 during an attack on the Marches overseen by Rhys ap Gruffydd. It was recaptured probably in 1195 by Marcher forces. The castle was again captured and destroyed in 1196 by Rhys ap Gruffydd. It was taken by the king, probably without resistance in 1208, when its lord, William Braose, was exiled. It was subsequently taken by Braose forces in 1215 and destroyed by King John on 2 August 1216. Rebuilt by Reginald Braose c.1218, it was captured and destroyed again by Llywelyn ab Iorwerth in 1231. Rebuilt by Richard, Earl of Cornwall in 1233-5, it was captured and destroyed by Llywelyn ap Gruffydd in 1264. Rebuilt by Roger Mortimer c.1265, it saw service during the war with Owain Glyn Dwr.

After the battle of Pilleth on 22 June 1402, royal garrisons were put into Clifford and Radnor castles. Sir John Greyndour of

Abenhall, Gloucestershire, was in command of Radnor Castle in person from August 1402 until March 1404, when his command was moved first to the Three Castles in Monmouthshire and then to Aberystwyth. As Brecon was besieged the garrison of Radnor had been tripled to more than 70 men on 24 June, 1403, and on 24 January, 1404, the garrison was again augmented. During the period between late July 1402, when the royal garrison was inaugurated, until January, 1405, almost £900 was spent in defending the castle. Then the government sought to privatize the war effort to allay some of the costs and appointed Richard Grey of Codnor to Radnor Castle, granting him the profits of the surrounding lordships and all the fines, ransoms and perquisites of war. With this act the history of the defence of Radnor slips from view. The castle was probably finally destroyed around 1645.

The castle at New Radnor consists of a ringwork, with a bailey to the north and west, and possibly further outworks north of this. The town walls enclosed the land to west, south and possibly east of the castle. No masonry of the castle still stands, although the remaining earthworks and foundations show that the castle was remodelled on several occasions, and this goes some way to supplement the recorded history of the site.

The main feature of the castle now, as in the Middle Ages, is the formidable ringwork. This is an irregularly shaped, deeply ditched platform, dominating the town. There is an interesting drawing cum plan of Radnor town and castle made by John Speed in 1610, some eighty years after the castle was noted as being out of repair, with the exception of the gatetower. It shows the castle with the main defences still standing to the height of the battlements, though no buildings appear to remain inside the enceinte—the line of the enclosing fortifications. Speed's other plans of castles are known to be remarkably accurate, and therefore we can reconstruct the castle defences as they were at the end of the Middle Ages: the ward consisted of a stone curtain of a roughly parallelogram shape. Towards the bailey, at the apexes of the ringwork, stood large, possibly square towers, whilst on the more defensible town side the facing towers can be seen to be round. However, it is more probable that they are all D–shaped as only the rear of the northern towers can be seen and only the fronts of the southern ones. The large

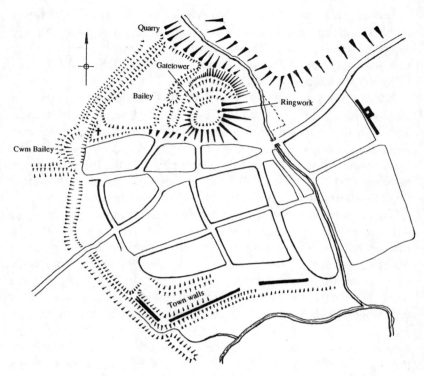

Quarry

Gatetower

Bailey

Cwm Bailey

Ringwork

Town walls

Plan showing the castle and town layout at New Radnor

tower to the north east is certainly D–shaped as its existing foundations demonstrate. The mortar in these remains is still hard and has
much gravel and lime in it. This tends to confirm that the castle was
demolished and robbed rather than that it collapsed.

It is possible that the main tower or keep, if there was one, was
that to the south-west which appears to overlook a castle gateway
on Speed's plan. The entrance here was a simple opening in the
curtain, facing towards the church. There is still a steep pathway
leading up to the site of this gate, but it is surely too steep to have
been the original entrance. More likely it is a quicker access route
to the jail, made in late medieval days, for which we have accounts
speaking of a gatetower cum prison. Obviously this simple gateway
does not fit the bill. The gatehouse proper was undoubtedly sited in
the tower at the northern apex of the site, and consequently allowed

access to and from the main ward. The site of the gatetower is now much disturbed and little can be said of it, other than the site suggests it was square. These gatetowers tend to be seen as early features, such as those at Exeter, Devon (c.1080) and Plessis Grimoult, Orne (destroyed 1047).

Speed shows no baileys to the north of the inner ward, and it must therefore be presumed that these were deserted by this date. The interior of the inner ward is now much disturbed due to an attempt to erect a monument in honour of Wellington here in the early nineteenth century, and it seems likely that the lowering of the rampart at the gatehouse site and the path up through the ditch, complete with circular projection, relate to this operation.

To the north and south, some 2m down the rampart, are traces of what may have been mantlet walls—low defensive walls protecting the rampart—or something to do with stone-robbing operations. Mantlet walls are more common in Europe, or at least have survived more, but similar defences may have existed at Painscastle some 12 miles to the south and a mantlet wall certainly surrounded the exposed side of the motte at Kingsland Castle, Herefordshire. However, this was set in the ditch and not on the rampart. Consequently it is possible that both these features at Radnor are the remains of robber trenches. Similar trenches can be seen on the motte on Ewias Harold, Herefordshire. Another possibility is that this feature is merely the original berm of the castle, the main rampart being the turf covered remains of the curtain wall. This interpretation certainly fits the remains at Radnor, although only trial excavation could prove the point.

Moving north from the site of the gatetower there is a double ditch with an intervening rampart. The outer ditch appears incomplete, though this may be due to it being filled in later, rather than being left unfinished. Beyond these ditches is the bailey. There is no trace of an original entrance to this ward, the present entrance through Mutton Dingle at the north-east corner being undoubtedly relatively modern. However, there are structures just beyond this part of the bailey which are not readily explained. There is what looks like a natural outcrop of rock that stands where a curtain or town wall would be expected, and the course of a newly laid drainage ditch has uncovered what appears to be the foundations of a 2m thick curtain wall in alignment with the previous feature. Below this, towards the site of the alleged 'Mutton Dingle' entrance, are the foundations of a rectangular stone structure, some 3m by 4.5m across, of uncertain date and purpose. Similar structures of one storey still exist in better condition some 15m to the north. It appears that these 'sheds' were something to do with the quarry alleged to be at this part of the site. If this is so, the Mutton Dingle gate then becomes, not a medieval entrance to the castle, but the easiest available access for stone-robbers to get to the site. Taken together it seems most likely that the entrance on to the ward has been disturbed by the rebuilding of the church.

The main ward is a peculiar oblong shape being some 55m deep by 137m long. It would appear that it was originally more of a traditional rectangular bailey, but the later double ditching of the ringwork caused a reduction in size. This ward is only obviously walled on its north front, where the low rampart masks the remains of a curtain wall some 1.8m thick. There is a slight rampart to the south-east of this ward that runs in front of the outer ditch, rising into a considerable, and militarily most irregular, rampart at the south-western extreme of the ward. It is possible that this feature is connected with the unfinished nature of the ditch here, but would be a most unlikely spoil heap. It is almost impossible to say what lay in the southern half of this bailey, due largely to the damage apparently done when it was reduced by the digging (or attempted digging if it was never completed) of the outer ditch around the ringwork, possibly during the 1233 rebuilding. What is noticeable is the marked rise in the ground in front of the two causeways over this ditch which may be some form of barbican. On the other side of the bailey, set inside the northern curtain, are traces of a large rectangular building, which appears to have been sub–divided and was possibly the hall or a court house. There also appears to be an internal square tower, which is normally seen as an early feature, (cf. Launceston, Cornwall). The curtain behind this structure can be seen running down the scarp of the bailey towards Cwm Bailey where it fades out. Another rampart can be seen breaking away from this continuation at the western apex of the ward, and gently curving back along the western extreme of the ward platform. This may possibly mark the extent of the bailey. It is difficult to say what happened at the south-west end of this bailey. Possibly the building of the Victorian church in the 1840s disturbed the defences and obscured the original entrance, although the rectangular structure could be the remains of a gatehouse. There is no trace of a curtain at the west end of the bailey, but to the east there is much rubble in the face of the irregular scarp of the ward, and it may be that this is the robbed-out remnants of a curtain, further damaged by the later road driven up Mutton Dingle.

Beyond the main bailey to the north is an outer ward, which recently was known as the Green Bailey or Beili Glas, although both wards may have been called this. Between the Green Bailey and the main ward is a set of triple ramparts (including the ward 'curtain') with a double ditch in between. The ramparts (apart from the main ward one) are now between 0.6m and 1.5m high and very narrow. Examination of where sheep tracks cut into them, and probable drainage ditches cut through them, strongly suggests that they cover stone walls of late medieval date and it is possible, though unlikely, that they may be either a pair of mantlet walls or another robber trench. This feature is most unusual and is not echoed at any other known Marches site. The central rampart is a continuation from that at the quarry, and several breaks in its structure suggest that it hides a stone wall some 1.2 to 1.5m thick, the minimum thickness that castle walls appear to have been built. This runs along the top of the ward ditch for its entire north front, and ends abruptly with the ditch it masks at the peculiar Cwm Bailey. This 'bailey' is undoubtedly an early feature, as can be demonstrated by the way the later outer rampart of the castle defences circumnavigates it to the north and west. Yet what is the purpose of this small quarry? The waterworks set in it may suggest that it was once a well or the site of a spring, but why set it on the periphery of the defences like this? Set into the top slope of this feature are what appears to be the rubble remains of the footings of the central rampart wall. This can be seen to follow the contours of Cwm Bailey. It is possible that this is just bedrock (the rock is very friable), but as it continues from the end of the central rampart this may be indicative of it having been a wall, though no mortar was found in the structure.

External to the central rampart, along the entire northern front, is a shallow ditch and then another rampart, which also shows some signs of having been a wall, though not as clearly as the inner two ramparts. This feature is first noticed some 6m north of the 'quarry face' and runs south-west to join up with the central rampart ditch. From here it follows the rampart and ditch closely until it reaches the Cwm Bailey. Here it turns and begins to circumnavigate this feature, until half-way down the slope it suddenly breaks off at a right angle and strikes across a field to a south running stream draining the high ground to the north. Here it fades out suddenly. There is a ditch south of this rampart and a counterscarp rampart beyond it. This parallels the main rampart back to Cwm Bailey where it dog-legs back onto the original course of the outer rampart, and probably proceeds south as the town wall. The site of the town wall can be picked up again east of the stream flowing down the ditch to the Summergill Brook.

Many features of Radnor Castle are of uncertain date and origin and it is likely that only excavation will enable them to give up their secrets. What can be stated is that the initial mound/ringwork is almost certainly of eleventh century date, as is the extent of the bailey, although many of its features are later. It is almost impossible to offer any date for the masonry remains, other than that they were most likely built before 1300. The plan and existing remains suggest an early origin, but this cannot be substantiated. It would seem likely that the castle became virtually obsolete after the conquest of Wales, and therefore most of the castle defences predate this time. The castle was said to have been destroyed in 1264 and this may indicate that what remains is of a later building. However, the destruction of 1264 may simply have been the firing of the wooden parts of the building—the stone walls may have survived intact. The plan provided for this castle may date to the 1233 rebuilding, or even earlier in the twelfth century. The suggested square gatetower supports an early date for the masonry defences, but it should be remembered that there are always precursors of a general trend in construction, and indeed later throwbacks.

In the new church beside the castle are the tombs of a knight with a round shield and his lady. As round shields are unusual it is possible that this knight was the crusader, Philip Braose, one of the first lords of the castle.

Barland Castle

Stepped mound

Motte

Road

A mound and bailey with slight evidence of stone defences
Location: Lies beside a no through road to
Burfa and Barland (SO 281 618)
Access: Is on private land, but can be seen from the top of stone
steps leading to a small gate on the roadside bank

Barland was undoubtedly one of the 'major' fortresses of Radnor
Lordship, and its Norman tenurial history starts before William
Braose gained possession of Radnor around 1095. At Domesday
two hides were held at Barland (*Bernaldeston*) from Hugh L'Asne
by one Thorkell. There was also a large unsized wood and a hay (an
area enclosed with a hedge or fence). The rest was waste. This land
was passed on to Philip Braose on Hugh's death after 1100.
Probably after 1165 William Braose granted Barland to the
Peytevin family (possibly later known as the Poitevins). In both
c.1137-9 and c.1160-70 the vill was noted as demesne land of, in

other words owned by, William Braose as the Lord of Radnor. However, by 1211-12 Barland was held by one Simon Cook. This was possibly as a result of the temporary deposition of some of the Braose retainers due to the Braose revolt of 1207-10, for by the time of the Crown's inquisition of 1304 into the Mortimer land-holdings, Barland was held by John le Peytevin for a ¼ knight's fee. It is most interesting to note that the Barland ¼ fee was buttressed by a further ¾ of a fee at Twyford (SO 396 591) making the whole worth 1 fee. Can Barland therefore be seen as a fortress with its appurtenant hinterland safe to the east? The evidence from Burfa, Womaston, Evenjobb and Newcastle might well support this. The tenurial evidence therefore suggests that Barland Castle was founded in the period after 1165 by the Peytevins, after the 2 hides of Barland had ceased to be the demesne of the Braoses. At the same time it was probably associated with Twyford near Leominster which, in a more secure area, could supply the needs of the castle and help support its upkeep.

Barland Castle is the furthest east of the castles in Radnor Lordship. It is set on a ridge-end site in a highland position in the hills that mark the present border between England and Wales. The remains are on a slight spur between two overshadowing hillsides, making the site peculiar in the extreme and probably militarily indefensible. This may suggest that Barland was more of a hunting lodge or mansion than a fully fledged castle.

Although the remains have long been classified as a motte and bailey, a close investigation indicates that the roughly 3m high 'motte' is in fact the collapsed remnants of a rectangular tower, the south and east walls of which can still be made out in the mound's side where sheep have disturbed the surface. This would probably have been the keep, set as it is in the least assailable part of the enceinte. A curtain wall abutted this tower and enclosed the roughly rectangular ward. In the north-eastern corner of the site the foundations of this curtain can still be traced, as also can the foundations of an apparently rectangular building that lay alongside it. The north-east corner of this curtain is chamfered, and no flanking can be traced. Crop marks along the northern face of the ditch that cuts the ward off from the slightly rising ground to the north indicates that the curtain wall continued along to the elongated stepped

The 'motte' from the ward

mound at the north-western corner. Here the ditch has been obscured by the metalled road that passes alongside the bailey, though no damage appears to have been done to the foundations of the curtain. The stepped mound is a most curious structure which apparently covers the remains of the curtain wall. This seems likely if the wall was not demolished at this point but has collapsed, forming a pile of its own debris, in a similar manner to the keep. However, this mound may have been altered or even created by the making of the road. The southern curtain of the bailey is not traceable, but judging from a slight ridge in the ground appears to have formed a right-angle. There is no trace of an entrance, but presumably this was to the north, for the apparent access to the south by the side of the keep leads to far too steep an incline down to the valley bottom below. An alternative suggestion is that the entrance lay to the west under the present road.

The plan of this small irregular enclosure castle on the Welsh frontier puts it into a small class that finds similarities in the early castles of St Briavels, Lydney, Newcastle Bridgend and Dinas Powys. These other castles seem to have been built reasonably early in the period 1067 to 1200. It is prudent with the dating evidence available to place Barland into a category of 1165 to 1200, suggesting that this castle was a 'throw back' to a more primitive design. Alternatively it is possible that it was built before 1104 by Hugh L'Asne.

Burfa and Womaston

A medium sized motte with slight traces of a bailey
Location: Within a marshy nature reserve (SO 276 611)
Access: A path leads across the nature reserve and through the site

Moated medium sized motte with traces of a now built upon bailey
Location: In the grounds of Womaston School, north of the
Hindwell Brook (SO 268 606)
Access: A private path leads through a gateway in the stone wall
which circles the site along the road and this passes the motte

The tenurial history of Burfa and Womaston probably dates to the time soon after Domesday when this fee was carved out of the 15 hides that made up the 1086 vill of Radnor. Burfa (*Burchoure*) was first mentioned in the 1211-12 survey of Radnor Barony carried out at the instructions of King John when it was held at a ¼ knight's fee by an unnamed knight. This fee seems to have included Womaston and Walton at an early date. By 1304 it had been absorbed by Ralph St Ouen into his fief of Burlingjobb at 1 knight's fee. Womaston is not mentioned in the early surveys and, being 'joined' with Burfa before 1304, suggests that the tenurial family had become extinct at an early date. Consequently, it is suggested that Burfa and Womaston castles were built simultaneously, probably soon after 1086. At some date the Burlingjobb fee had Burton Court, in Herefordshire, attached to it, which with Burfa, Walton and Womaston made a total of 1 knight's fee. It cannot be demonstrated that Burfa and Womaston castles were linked with other, more peaceful and perhaps profitable lands to the east, though Burton Court may have been such a land.

Burfa Castle seems to have been a polygonal enclosure castle, although it is now too badly damaged to be certain. The main feature is the mutilated motte, standing some 4.5m above the bailey platform which appears to lie to the north. The motte has a surface area some 18m in diameter and would have dominated the marshy land to the north, west and south. It is probable that Womaston Castle, just 1 mile to the west, would have been visible from here. It

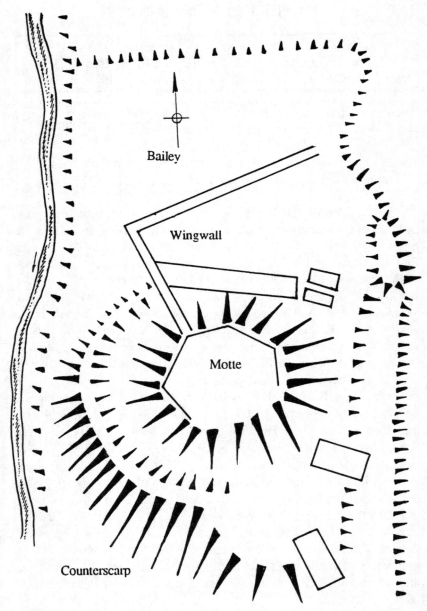

Bailey

Wingwall

Motte

Counterscarp

Plan of Burfa Castle

is likely that Burfa motte was crowned with a polygonal shell keep of which traces could be seen until recently in the badly damaged southern face. Here the motte appears to have been cut away, possibly to allow two later rectangular buildings to be built. The roughly 0.75m thick rubble remains of the foundations of these buildings still survive. Much of the rubble, and probably also that from the keep, is strewn about the base of the motte. Coming down from the motte to the north-west are slight traces of a wingwall. This apparently makes an acute junction with a narrow rectangular foundation. It is possible that this is the remnant of an original external stair, or forebuilding, to the keep. However, the wingwall appears to continue north-west, as a crop mark, for some 3m before making a right-angled turn and heading to a depression at the side of the road that eats into the flat platform on this side of the castle. This continuation of the wingwall may have been the bailey wall, even though it now only appears as a crop mark and a very slight ridge in the field. If this is not the extent of the bailey then it may possibly be marked by the line of small trees (quite likely an over-grown hedge) and slight rise in the ground further to the north. Where this rise meets the small stream north-north-west of the motte a faint depression can be seen which may have once been a ditch. Whatever the case, the bailey defences do not appear to have been substantial. To the south of the keep it is likely that there was a wingwall similar to that to the north, though all trace of this has been removed by the later mutilation of this side of the motte. As the 'Ditch Mill' of the 1304 survey would seem to be immediately south of the motte, it is possible that the two rectangular structures disturbing this part of the site formed part of the mill buildings, or were even a later house or farm buildings.

On the west side of the motte, outside the postulated bailey defences, a low counterscarp bank encircles this half of the mound. Despite being in such a lowland position with the motte being set on a quite noticeable low rise, it would appear that this relatively narrow ditch, some 3.5m wide, was always dry. To the north-east of the motte is a large oblong mound full of rubble which may be a spoil heap, rather than part of the castle. However, it should be noted that between this structure and the motte there is a disturbed area that appears to take the shape of two rectangular pits. It is possible that these represent basements of the entrance to the keep. Certainly, it appears to be roughly central in the bailey. A carved quoin, with diagonal tooling, of what was probably a window or door arch was discovered lying in the ditch bottom. Such a stone is generally assigned to a relatively early date.

To the east of the oblong mound a metalled road cuts roughly north-south across the site, probably through the bailey, although it is possible that it occupies the former bailey ditch. A little to the east is a stream and then, further away, Offa's Dyke which cuts across the slope of the hill on which stands the Iron Age Burfa Camp.

The design of this masonry motte and bailey is that of a relatively early Norman castle, indicating that it may have been preceded by an earth and timber castle in the first few years of Radnor Lordship. As such it would seem likely that it was transformed with the addition of a stone keep and polygonal curtain walls in the twelfth century. The curious shape of the long building north of the motte may also suggest an early date. It probably began to decay in the aftermath of the loss of its knightly lord, sometime in the period 1211 to 1304, though it may have been used as the caput (the centre of the fee) of the St Ouen family after the loss of their Norman lands in 1204/5.

Womaston, the other castle of the fief, is set in low lying, probably once marshy land, close to the Summergill Brook. Set in such a position it is not surprising to find wet defences were utilized here. The central feature of the site was, and still is, the 3m high moated mound on or around which the keep once stood. Evidence for the foundations of a polygonal shell keep, the walls of which were some 1.8m in thickness, can still be found some 0.3m under the current surface, whilst part is exposed to the north of the mound where a recent tree fall has ripped up the covering earth. The mound sides are still very steep and it is possible that the keep was originally commenced at, or near, ground level, and that the mound was originally built up inside it. Surrounding the keep was a moat probably about 3m wide and at least 1.8m deep. This is still in evidence and mostly water-filled, even in the driest of summers.

It is now difficult to discern the extent of the castle's bailey even though the northern defences are quite evident. The modern pond,

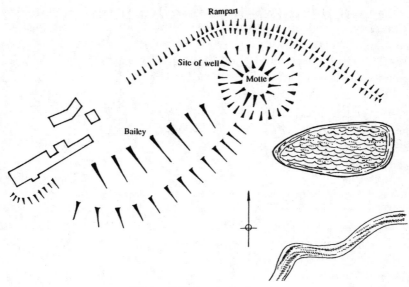

Plan of Womaston Castle

with a sluice between the motte and the brook, may have occupied the site of an original ditch. Running from just north of this pond is a rampart that reaches up to 1.2m high that corners the motte, on which remnants of stone walling can be seen protruding, especially around the motte. It would appear likely that this is the remnant of the bailey curtain wall. Any ditch that was in front of this has since been filled by the metalled road to the east and a hard packed farm track to the north. There is what may be a ploughed out rampart running from the motte moat south-westwards towards the brook. It then appears to curve gently upwards towards the modernized farm buildings which may overlie the original entrance to the site. The bailey has a gentle slope down to the brook. On the 1:2500 OS map a well is shown immediately north-east of the motte moat. The plan of this castle appears to be somewhat similar to its near neighbour at Burfa, although the shell keep there does not appear to have had a wet moat. A keep with wet defences is also similar to that found at Kinnerton and just possibly Nimble and Knapp. It would there-fore seem best to also assign an early date to Womaston Castle. Both Burfa and Womaston may have remained in occupation during the tenure of the St Ouen family in the thirteenth century.

Castell Nimble and Old Radnor Castle

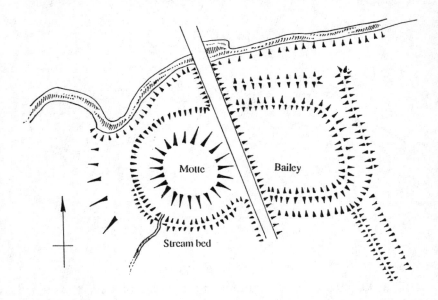

A low mound and weak bailey, surrounded by dry moats
Location: In the fields north of Old Radnor (SO 248 594)
Access: A public footpath which leads downhill from opposite the
church passes through the site

A dry moated site
Location: Behind Old Radnor church car park (SO 250 590)
Access: Can be seen from the church car park

Nimble Castle is a most peculiar site set beside a stream called
Riddings Brook. It is classified as a motte and bailey yet its remains
are insignificant; the so–called 'motte' being only some 0.6m above
ground level. This has some rubble spread around the surface of the
mound and may possibly have supported a polygonal shell keep,
built up from the bed-rock. This mound, like many others, may
therefore be the debris which has accumulated over the remnants of
fallen stonework, rather than being a defensive structure in its own

right. This castle has in antiquity been described as the predecessor of New Radnor Castle, but this is stated without any substantiating evidence.

The likelihood of stone defences is strengthened by the fact that the site would appear totally indefensible without substantial walls. A ring of approximately two hundred year old trees stand only around the edge of the mound, perhaps favouring a place where they can feed upon the lime in the old mortar of the probable shell keep. The ditch surrounding the mound is only 0.9m deep and 3m across. There is a slight counterscarp bank to the south which is broken to allow access for a stream bed. The bailey is separated from the mound by a dirt track consisting of packed rubble that probably fills the old mound ditch to the east. The bailey has the slightest of ramparts on all sides bar the road, though it is strongest to the south and east. It seems best to interpret this as the turfed-over remnants of a curtain though only excavation could prove the point. Surrounding the bailey on the downhill north and east sides is a counterscarp bank, that to the north being virtually level with the silted ditch bottom. This bank has been broken through at its north-eastern apex, no doubt for the draining of the moat which appears just as insubstantial as the one around the mound. From the south-east corner of the site a rampart and shallow ditch runs off at a near right angle towards the church on the hill a quarter of a mile away. The church itself probably does not date from earlier than the thirteenth century, although the font is much older. If the two sites are connected, as the rampart seems to suggest, then it is possible that Castell Nimble, with its flimsy defences, was occupied contemporaneously.

The curious 'moated site' at Old Radnor, damaged by the building of the school on its north–eastern front in the last century, is also a peculiar earthwork. It is now, due perhaps to the building work, D–shaped and, unlike Castell Nimble, deeply ditched, no doubt due to its highland, rather than water–logged, setting. No trace of masonry has been found anywhere on the site and the well set in the bottom of the ditch must surely date to a period after the site's military use.

Opinions as to the castle's origin vary from pre-1066 Welsh to a fourteenth century fortified parsonage similar to others in

Montgomeryshire. As Old Radnor was not the precursor of New Radnor a late date is more likely. However, Old Radnor could be the 'successor' of the nearby Walton of the 1304 survey, at a time when the heavy rain and floods recorded during the reign of Edward II may have made the lower lying lands untenable.

Evenjobb castles

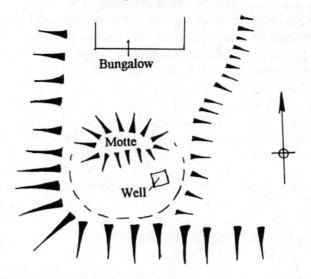

A heavily damaged motte, where remains of a shell keep
have been made into a rockery
Location: At the northern apex of the road junction in
Evenjobb (SO 263 624)
Access: On private land and not easily seen

A low mound in a marshy moat
Location: Part of a farmyard to the north-east of
Evenjobb (SO 266 625)
Access: A public footpath next to the old school at the
north-east corner of the village leads past the site

Evenjobb would appear to have been created early as a fee of
Radnor lordship, and it would seem likely that Aston (SO 462 625)
was also attached to the fief to make a $\frac{1}{2}$ knight's fee. In 1211-12,
this fee was held by a knight who's name was not recorded.
Possibly he was in disgrace or a state of rebellion with his Braose
lords. The 1304 enquiry of the Mortimer landholdings found
Evenjobb and Aston held by William Fousel for a half fee.

The remains of two possible castles are found in the near vicinity of Evenjobb. What may be the first castle is a heavily damaged motte and probable bailey (SO 263 624); the remains of the motte lie at the apex of a road junction. The bailey probably lay to the north and is now under a bungalow and its garden. What is left of the motte is made of a rich loam, some three-quarters of which has recently been removed, probably for road workings in the early 1980s. The remnants of the mound have now been converted into a pleasing rockery, but traces of the internal wall of a polygonal shell keep can still be seen in its southern face. This apparently revetted, or faced, the mound in a roughly 15m diameter wall. In the eastern portion of the motte site is a capped well, which could have supplied the occupants of the keep. Other than this little now remains. A hedge can be seen running eastward from the site towards the second castle (SO 266 625) and it is possible that the hedge lies upon a very slight ridge which may be the remains of a rampart and palisade connecting the two sites. Certainly they are in sight of one another. Immediately to the west of the castle was an earthen dam (SO 261 625) that was probably part of a mill complex of unknown date.

The second, possibly later, site (SO 266 625) is set at the confluence of two streams, which added to the castle's defensibility. The 'motte' is towards the west of the site and commands both the bailey and the site of the modern village to the south and southwest. To the north is a gentle rise, but no bailey defence has been found on this side. A rectangular platform at the eastern extreme of the site is apparently an old silage pit. The two streams converging at the site cut deep ditches into the loam and clay, which when water–filled must have presented a formidable obstacle. To fill these ditches with water a powerful earth and masonry dam was built across the confluence of the two streams. This is now breached and clearly shows its earthen construction. In the dam's western half two sluices with finely carved quoins were visible until ten years ago, but they have now been removed or otherwise destroyed, although their position is still apparent. Between here and the 'motte' the marshy ground, which is largely silt, has been extensively altered in the past 100 years by waterworks for the school house below. The original entrance to the site was probably

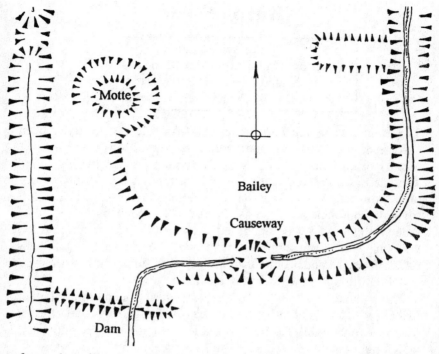

from the vill where the modern causeway crosses the southern ditch.

The low 1.2m 'motte' is some 9m in diameter and is set in its own now heavily silted moat. The mound is full of stone and may be the collapsed remains of a round tower rather than a motte. Although there is much rubble in the bailey edge as well as along the ditch, no trace of a curtain wall has been discovered, though one would have been sensible to protect the bailey from the nearby high ground to the east. The site has undoubtedly been long abandoned, but no date can be suggested. The possible round or polygonal tower may indicate a later rather than an earlier date, although the Normans were building such towers from the earliest days in Normandy and it is likely that they did the same on this side of the Channel. However, it is possible that the entire site is non–military and was concerned wholly with water power. The lack of a northern defensive line may further support the idea of a non-military occupation.

Knapp Farm

An impressive mound
Location: On the north side of the A44 at
Knapp Farm (SO 246 600)
Access: Can be clearly seen from the A44

The mound at Knapp Farm is an odd affair. It has generally been classified as a mutilated motte, although suggestions made include that its origins may be a prehistoric tumulus or a windmill knap. The site has no recorded history and the mound is certainly disfigured from heavy afforestation. The felling of these trees has left several prominent pock marks. In one of these a stone roof tile of indeterminate date was found, but whether this was anything to do with the site is questionable. However, the bricks and builder's rubble found in and around the base suggests dumping has occurred and the infilling of the ditch if one existed.

The mound now has a definite east-west orientation. Whether this is caused by mutilation to the site or whether this is an original feature is uncertain. To the north is a small stream, presently dry, which may once have fed any water defences. On the southern side the A44 has destroyed any potential defences. The broken ground to the west of the mound also appears to have suffered from tipping as there is much extraneous material in the ground. It is also possible that the farm to the east of the mound overlays part, if not all, of the bailey. It is common to find continuity of site usage through the ages and the farm may be the descendant of the original castle buildings, the defences being allowed to decay as the frontier became more peaceable. Further earthworks have been suggested under and south of the A44. However, the large number of tumuli nearby may mark this out as a major prehistoric site.

Kinnerton Castle

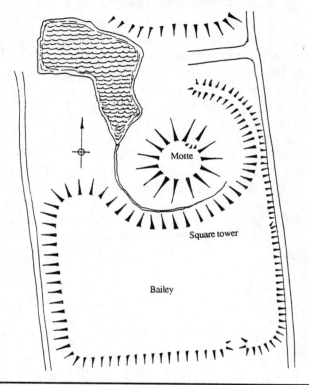

An impressive motte with a moat
Location: In Kinnerton village (SO 245 630)
Access: Visible from the road around Kinnerton Chapel,
with a Georgian house on the bailey

Kinnerton is one of the few vills in the lordship of Radnor that is actually mentioned in the early part of the Middle Ages, although it is not referred to in any of the surveys before that of the Mortimer landholdings of 1304. On 31 May, 1252, Henry III passed a royal writ in favour of one Margeria the daughter of Isolda after holding an inquisition into the rights of Radnor Lordship. We have no knowledge of Margeria's mother Isolda, but it seems likely that she held 3½ virgates of land with appurtenances in the vills of Radnor and Kinnerton. On her death sometime before 1252, Roger

Mortimer of Wigmore (1246-82), as lord of Radnor, granted this land to one William Fitz Elye together with 'other' unknown persons. Margeria took out a writ at the king's court for her rights to the land and as a result of the king's enquiry it was decreed that the royal writ ran into Mortimer's Marcher Barony of Radnor as a part of Herefordshire. Presumably Margeria got her justice for nothing more is heard of the dispute.

Unfortunately this tells us little of the castle itself. It would seem possible that it was a demesne castle of the lord of Radnor, but if so why did the lords need to retain a castle so near to their caput, or centre of their fee, at Radnor? Perhaps it was an early tenurial castle whose knight had no heir and the castle and its appurtenances reverted to the lord of Radnor. Alternatively it may have been built by one of the ancestors of Isolda.

The castle appears to have stood in a naturally wet site. The motte is now the main feature, standing 4.5m high and which helps to block the access from the higher ground to the north, making the castle another typical ridge-end site as so often occurs in this border region. Obviously choosing such a site made the castle semi-defensible from the outset. The mound has recently been mutilated, especially to the north and east, probably by the uprooting of trees. The exposed fill consists of much gravelly material, but without masonry or rubble, although, judging from other sites, a polygonal shell keep could be expected. The slight platform seen at the motte bottom to the south could mark the original entrance to the keep, but is more likely to be further tree damage. A crop mark and slight ridge suggests a 4.5m square tower at the south quadrant of the motte, though this might well be a post-castle structure. The mound is still surrounded by a ditch from which a small stream flows into the pond to the north-west which may be a contraction of the original water defences. To the north is a counterscarp bank similar to, but in a better condition than that at Burfa. The bailey appears to be roughly rectangular, but it too has been much mutilated. Metalled roads surround the site to east, south and west and it is possible that another bailey lay under the present house and garden to the south. Certainly the 'sunken trackways' surrounding this portion of the site point to such a scenario. The southern 'entrance' to the bailey is almost certainly a modern disfiguration, as is the cut to the east.

Newcastle or Evancoyd House Castle

A low mound with a house on the site of the possible bailey
Location: To the west of the B4357 through
Evancoyd (SO 261 632)
Access: On private land

About a mile to the north of Evenjobb lies Evancoyd House motte set on the summit of a ridge overlooking the road to Cascob, Discoed and Pilleth. It is possible that this is the 'Newcastle' founded between 1135 and 1211. In the 1211-12 survey the $\frac{1}{4}$ fee at 'Newcastle' was held by William les Yveteaux who had probably had this fee granted to him from the fee of Evenjobb. Why this vill had been sub-divided is unknown, but this may have been a military measure taken in the aftermath of Cadwallon ap Madog's rising supremacy in the district prior to 1179. This little castle and its appurtenances may therefore have been placed to block the entrance from a Welsh mountain routeway into the Radnor Plain from Maelienydd. To Newcastle fee was added the $\frac{1}{4}$ fee of Hinton (SO 410 598) as an appurtenance—no doubt for the castle's better sustenance.

The mound now rises only some 1.5m above ground level, and it seems likely that this is its original height. There is now no trace of a ditch although there is room for one. Roughly 9m in surface diameter this motte appears to have once supported, or more likely to have been enclosed by, a polygonal shell keep, slight traces of which are apparent to the east where farm buildings have encroached on the site. Another ring of trees is seen 'leaching' the lime from the probable masonry. To the east of the motte lies a small stone-built house, undoubtedly on the site of the former bailey. In the garden west of the house a slight rampart probably marks the extent of this ward. However, this could have been formed during the construction of the modern waterworks a short distance away. A track to the south of the site may mark the bailey ditch.

Dinieithon

A low motte surrounded by a shallow ditch
Location: 2km south of Crossgates (SO 092 630)
Access: On private land, but visible from the public footpath
on the west bank of the Eithon

The castle was built between 1093/5 by Ralph Mortimer and probably destroyed in 1134/6 by Madog ab Idnerth, although it was possibly rebuilt by his son Cadwallon around 1165. It is not mentioned after Cadwallon's death in 1179 and by 1242 was certainly succeeded by Cefnllys.

To consolidate his gains in Maelienydd in 1093-5, Ralph Mortimer of Wigmore is claimed in the Mortimer family history to have built a castle called Dinieithon, which formed the centre of his new lordship and which took its name from the commote in which it was built, as so often happened with early Norman castles in Wales. Therefore, the place to look for this castle is in the commote of Swydd Dinieithon, where there are only two castle sites: Cefnllys (SO 090 615), and, almost immediately beneath it, the suggestively named 'Old Castle' (SO 092 631). The latter is most likely to be the site of Dinieithon because of its strategic position, immediately above the main crossing over the River Eithon, together with its motte and bailey plan. In the thirteenth century Cefnllys is repeatedly referred to as being 'the new castle of Maelienydd', distinguishing it from the old one. This latter has to be identified with the site just beneath Cefnllys Hill.

The castle identified as Dinieithon appears to have been abandoned at an early date. It lies on a low rocky spur, which slopes gently down to the river on the west, and is protected by a steep scarp to the north-east. The innermost defence is a low clay-built motte, on the exposed three sides of which stands a three-quarter ringwork, appearing to consist of large fragments of shale and some exceedingly hard mortar. These three sides were additionally protected by a ditch, which is now but a shallow impression of its former self on all but its southern part, where it is still some 3m deep (and interspersed with rubble). This ditch was crossed by a causeway to the west. These remains suggest that the main defence at this castle consisted of a shell keep set on the low motte, the north eastern part of which has since collapsed down the steep scarp onto the flood plain below.

The inner bailey, which still existed in 1910, apparently followed the line of the slope of the hill, and formed an ellipse, with a bulge to the south, where there were the remains of an inturned gateway, and a few stones of the curtain. In the past ten years these features have been quarried away. Further south-west from the site of the gatehouse is a roughly rectangular platform which most likely formed an outer enclosure towards the loop of the Eithon.

Cymaron (and two possible siege castles)

One possible siege castle is in the rough ground on the other side of the river, the second is in the field above the castle

> Deeply ditched motte and a bailey with massive ramparts
> Location: 3km south-west of Llanbister Road
> railway station (SO 152 703)
> Access: Clearly visible from the minor road
> which passes under the ramparts

The castle was probably started together with Dinieithon in 1093/5 by Ralph Mortimer. By 1134 it had come into the hands of Pain fitz John when it was stormed and destroyed, probably by Madog ab Idnerth. It was rebuilt by Hugh Mortimer in 1144, but probably retaken by Cadwallon ap Madog around 1150. On Cadwallon's death in 1179 the castle was occupied by the sheriff of Hereford, but taken from him by Cadwallon's sons in 1182. Roger Mortimer expelled the sons of Cadwallon from the castle in 1195 and held it until 1215 when it was destroyed by Bishop Giles Braose of Hereford and Llywelyn ab Iorwerth. The castle was rebuilt by the Mortimers more as a manor house than a castle after 1240 and was still in use as a court as late as 1360.

Cymaron is another castle possibly built by Ralph Mortimer to secure his gains in Maelienydd, this one to control the commote of Swydd Rhiwallt. Its position is somewhat similar to that of Dinieithon, Cymaron occupying a spur of ground between the River Aran and one of its tributaries. At the exposed southern 'neck' of the spur, on which the castle is situated, is a natural 'motte', which appears to be a scarped lozenge-shaped solid rock outcrop. East of this is the roughly rectangular, ramparted inner ward, with what may be a modern break in the rampart to form an entrance to the north-east. Protecting this possible gateway is a further irregular enclosure, also with a probably modern inturned break in the rampart to the north-east, immediately overlooking the tributary of the Aran. Enclosing the site to the south and west is a great bank that must have offered the defenders some protection from the overlooking hills. This bank fades out towards the overlooking high ground to the north, though this may be caused by recent in-filling. The more impressive section of ditching appears to be a small quarry, at a point where there were supposed to have been buildings at the turn of the century. The rough broken ground to the west suggests traces of additional defences to the north to further isolate the castle from the dangerous higher ground. Certainly the defences on this front lack strength, which is peculiar on the exposed side. There may be a curtain wall buried in the northern inner ward rampart, which would have made the bailey much more defensible, but there is little other trace of this structure on the rest of the site, the rampart elsewhere consisting of a stone filling of water-rounded rubble and gravel.

The motte top is most uneven and may possibly never have been properly defended, or, more likely, is now greatly mutilated. The remains of a narrow wall, roughly 1.2m thick, can be traced running north to south across the motte top. Whether this was part of a medieval structure on the motte or a later building cannot be ascertained today. There are several large uncut pieces of rubble in the ditch between the motte and bailey. A collapse of the rampart at the north-western angle shows that there was no masonry set on or in advance of the bank. However, this does not rule out the possibility of a wall behind the rampart as has been suggested at Old Castleton, in Herefordshire. A ditch was found between the inner and outer baileys on the north-eastern side, but may have been filled in by the modern entrance track and barn on the other side. In the eastern half of the inner bailey are two fairly modern buildings, built of local rubble, but there is no trace of the courthouse that was once here. The impression is that the site was never of great military strength and it is no surprise that the castle became a backwater with the building of the major lordship castles in the 1240s.

Recently two possible siege castles have been discovered. About 100m west of the motte, at the top of the overshadowing ridge, is a small 6m high mound, cut into on the southern side, which appears to consist solely of natural rubbly shale. There is no trace of a ditch around the base of the mound, but a siege castle would not necessarily need a ditch. The other mound, which appears on aerial photographs to be far more like a motte, is on the south side of the River Aran overlooking the castle. If that to the west is an outpost of the castle, then that to the south could well be a siege castle, though whether Norman or Welsh is open to question.

Cefnllys

Looking over the rock cut ditch of the southern castle towards the northern castle 'motte'

A major castle covering the top of a hill in a loop of the
River Eithon, with impressive ditches
Location: 3km east of Llandrindod Wells (SO 088 614)
Access: A path leads up the hillside from Cefnllys Church,
itself reached by footpaths from each side of the Eithon

The castle was built in 1242 under the auspices of the eleven year old
Roger Mortimer. It was taken and destroyed in 1262 and not rebuilt
until 1268. Subsequently it was massively refortified in 1272/74, this
being the new work at the southern end of the hill. It was neverthe-
less taken at the end of 1294 when the last Brian Brampton may have
been killed here. It was rebuilt soon after and was probably unsuccessfully attacked by Glyn Dwr. It was still garrisoned in 1406 and
refurbished again in the 1430s. It was a ruin by 1588.

On the summit of Cefnllys Hill there are the remains of what
appear to be two separate castles, the earlier one being at the
northern end. This northern castle is an odd structure, the main
feature of which is what appears to be a 'motte' which forms an
irregular ellipse, with the angles running from east to west. If this

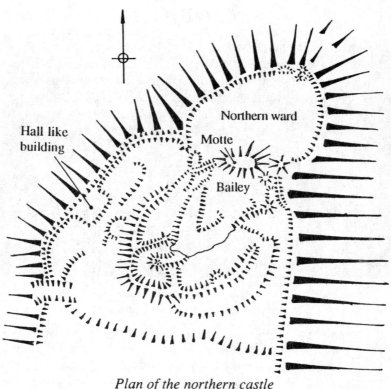

Plan of the northern castle

really is a motte it can probably be listed as the last known construction of such a military feature in England and Wales. Certainly, as a defensive feature it is not, and appears never to have been, very impressive. However, a recent survey has found traces of a rectangular keep, with forebuildings to both north and south, with a ramp on its south-western side. A supposed square tower is also suggested at the southern angle of the inner ward, overlying the outer defences where a rubble mound overlies the outer rampart. It seems most likely that this and the curiously-shaped 'motte' merely hide collapsed buildings, as did the mounds at Bleddfa and Cascob churches, which were long supposed to have been mottes, but in reality were simply the rubble of collapsed church towers.

Immediately to the east of this 'motte' are two small mounds, possibly the remnants of a tower, or of two small turrets. The bailey, of which these mounds form the north-eastern apex, is roughly triangular, and rubble mounds indicate that the main castle buildings lay against its internal wall. The entrance was probably at the southern end where a confusing, and possibly non-military series of causeways cross the ditch. Surrounding this now silted channel is a triangular counterscarp bank, which has a 'killing platform' on its south-eastern side. There is no space for such platforms on the other sides, where other structures apparently existed. The site was cut off from the rest of the hilltop by an escarpment, now breached at its south-eastern apex by the modern entrance to the hillfort site and which, judging by the defensive entrance to the north, is a late addition. On the fairly narrow western ledge between the inner ward and the scarp of the hill, is a long narrow ward, protected by a gate at its northern end, which was apparently overlooked by a tower in the walls enclosing the inner bailey. There are also the remains of a rectangular hall-like building in the western curtain. At the northern end of the site is a third and final entrance ward, which is directly overlooked and commanded by the 'motte'. An ancient track leads up to a complex gateway at the northern end, the track being overlooked by at least two tower platforms in the ward circuit. It would appear that entrance was originally gained through this gate, and then ran the entire length of the castle, to the entrance of the inner ward through its gate at the south end, thus exposing any attacker to the full defensive capabilities of the castle. It could well be that when the Welsh took the 'gatekeepers' of this castle by surprise in 1262 they came from the south, where only the now insignificant scarp kept them from the main entrance. An attack from the north would certainly have proved more difficult.

At the southern end of the hill is the later c.1273 castle which Roger Mortimer added to the defences after the Treaty of Montgomery in 1267. Under the treaty Mortimer was allowed to repair Cefnllys, but he also added this small square enclosure cut off from the rest of the hilltop to the north by a fine rock-cut ditch, and of which Llywelyn ap Gruffydd was to complain so bitterly in 1273/4 as being outside the terms of the treaty. The scattered foundations of the gatehouse now mark the only recognizable remains of the stone fortifications. The large collapsed mound in the centre probably indicates the remnants of a keep of some description,

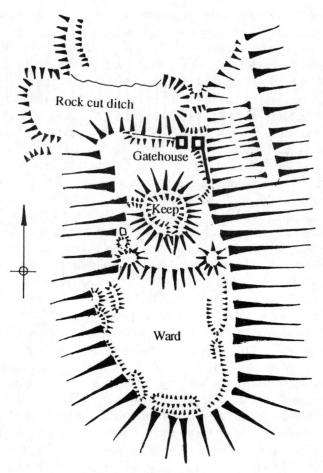

Plan of the southern castle

rather than a motte. Mounds to east and west probably also mark former towers, whilst traces of walls suggest that the curtain abutted onto the keep, making this structure part of the enceinte to east and west. Below the main ward to the south lies a further lightly defended ward.

It has been suggested that the castle was initially a hillfort. The hilltop ditches may support this theory, in which case the original construction work would date back to the Iron Age.

Knucklas

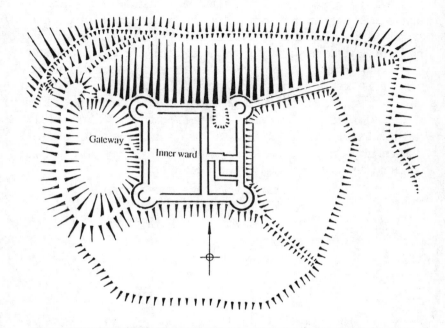

Gateway

Inner ward

Foundations of a stone building top what may be
an Iron Age hillfort
Location: On the north side of Knucklas village (SO 250 745)
Access: A footpath leads up the mound from the village

The castle was begun by Ralph Mortimer and finished by his son
Roger in 1242. It was surrendered through fear to the army of
Prince Llywelyn in December, 1262, and possibly never rebuilt,
although it was mentioned in the early fourteenth century. It
certainly did not exist as a castle by 1403.

The fortress at Knucklas shows some similarities to that at
Cefnllys, though it was not constructed on such a large scale. The
main defences, lying on the highest point of a large hilltop,
consisted of a small, roughly 15m square inner ward, which is
almost small enough to be classified as a 'keep'. Each of its four
corners was further protected by a small round tower. There was a

complex set of buildings at the eastern end of the fortress. To the west was an apparent barbican, but it has possibly been altered by later quarrying. The entrance lay on this western side, by a simple 'break in the wall' gateway. The northern side of the castle was protected by the steep scarp of the hill, the side from which the castle was probably approached. To the exposed south and east were large 'killing platforms'. The 'barbican' to the west may also have been such a platform though this is now difficult to judge. The rest of the hilltop was obviously fortified, possibly as a vill, but also possibly as a hillfort. A narrow path winds its way up the hill from the Knighton side to under the barbican. This may be the original entrance similar to the one found at Cefnllys.

Castell y Blaidd

Unfinished ringwork in a lofty position
Location: 3km north-east of Llanbadarn Fynydd
Access: Lies adjacent to a bridleway, but can be seen from the
gated road which leads onto the hills from Llanbadarn Fynydd

Castell y Blaidd is a most debatable site and is included in this survey because of its 'Castell' name. I am of the opinion that it is an early thirteenth century castle that was abandoned, incomplete, for the better site at Tinboeth, another high lying ringwork, commanding the upper reaches of the River Eithon. Tinboeth is clearly visible just over a mile away to the south-west.

Tinboeth was in operation as Roger Mortimer's castle of 'Dynbaud' in 1282, but was not mentioned amongst the many Mortimer castles which fell in 1262, or those that were held by Ralph Mortimer on his death in 1246. Roger Mortimer may well have been the founder of Tinboeth, for later his son appears as William Mortimer 'de chastel Tunbard'. As there is no written evidence for the foundation of Tinboeth (obviously a late Marcher castle) it may be that there was an equally obscure predecessor. Alternatives are that the site is early Norman, native Welsh, or prehistoric. All are possible.

Castell y Blaidd, or castle of the wolf as it translates from the Welsh, consists of a roughly horseshoe-shaped single rampart and ditch crowning a low hill at the end of a large meadow. It appears that either the ringwork was never completed or has been utterly destroyed to the west. The ditch is irregular to the north, while it is not even apparent to the west, which may support the view that the site was unfinished. The irregular, pocked nature of the interior may also support this view, or possibly that of a prehistoric origin. To the north lies what appears to be a pillow mound, or rabbit warren, some 16.5m by 4.5m, beyond which is a field bank. Continuing further beyond the bank, on the side of a rise opposite a deep gully are two roughly circular low banks which may have formed sheep or cattle corrals. Certainly the evidence seems to point to intense agricultural and other activity in this highland area over the millennia.

Tinboeth

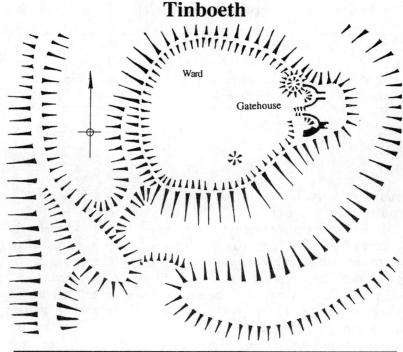

Ward

Gatehouse

A deep ditch surrounds the site and encloses the few shattered
remains of the castle walls on the hilltop
Location: 3km north-west of Llanbister (SO 090 755)
Access: By track and public footpath which sets off
opposite a lay-by on the A483

On 25 July, 1304, an inquisition found that in the cantref of
Maelienydd there was a castle at 'Dymbaud', but no town. The
castle was still functional in 1316 and in 1322 it was amongst those
Mortimer possessions that were surrendered to the king with the
disgrace of that family. This is its last mention as a functional
castle. Undoubtedly the successful conquest of Wales and the
security of the previously volatile Welsh Mortimer lands ended the
military purpose of this bleak fortress. As no civilian site was
formed around this isolated site, and there was no political reason
for its existence, abandonment and decay seem to have rapidly

followed, with the consequence that by Leland's day it was no more than 'greate ruines'. (See also Castell y Blaidd, the previous entry, for additional history.)

The castle occupies a large hilltop, which, like the other late Mortimer castles, may originally have been a hillfort. The main defence at Tinboeth consists of a small polygonal ward, 21m in diameter, which was fortified in stone. To the east lay what appears to have been a small double D-towered Edwardian gatehouse, with a barbican of some description. On the northern side of this is a deep circular depression, which may be the robbed out remains of a circular tower-keep. To the east is a further causeway that crossed the still impressive ditch, some 9m deep. Again flat 'killing plat-forms' lay to the exposed south and east sides where any attacking forces could be cut to pieces by fire from the curtain. The lack of any flanking towers again makes this site rather primitive, as all the later Mortimer castles appear to have been. The three deep gullies to the south of the site appear to be medieval open cast quarries, no doubt cut to provide the masonry for the castle.

Buddugre

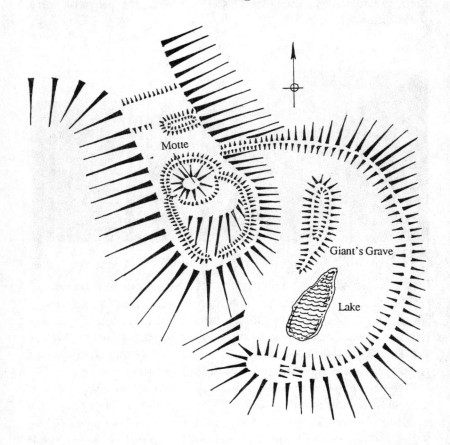

Motte

Giant's Grave

Lake

Eroded motte and bailey castle in a lofty position
Location: 3.5km south of Llanbister (SO 101 696)
Access: A public path leads to the castle from the farm
of the same name south of the site

At Buddugre, high above the Eithon valley, lies the eroded remains
of a motte and bailey castle. This castle, the chief, indeed, the only
fortress of the commote of Swydd Buddugre, was possibly the

The motte from the south

caput, or centre, of the early medieval princes of Maelienydd, and the indistinct kingdom of Cynllibiwg. Certainly its position and scale are indicative of this. It lay roughly in the centre of Maelienydd, protected from Norman incursions by the River Eithon, and some four miles from the new Cistercian abbey of Cwmhir founded by Cadwallon ab Madog.

The plan appears to have been very similar to that of a typical late eleventh century Norman castle. The large, low motte occupies a strong position towards the end of a long spur, dominating the valley below. The mound is surrounded by a shallow ditch, which is broken to east, west and south by causeways. To the north is a barely perceptible semi-circular counterscarp bank, whilst to the south, on ground which rapidly falls into a quite steep scarp, is a small rectangular bailey with rounded corners, which was once ramparted, but apparently never, or only extremely lightly, ditched. Entrance was gained by a simple break in the rampart, almost oppo- site the motte, and facing the approach up from the valley. Opposite this gate is a long spur which curves away to the east to form a semi-circle which almost joins up, in much reduced form, with the castle motte to the north. This appears to be a village enclosure,

*View from the bailey over the Giant's Grave and small lake,
indicating the hilltop position so favoured by the Welsh*

somewhat similar to that at Knucklas, though it is just possible that
both were single vallum hillforts. In the centre of this large enclosure are two distinct features—a small lake to the south, and a
largely quarried-out rock ridge (known as the Giant's Grave) to the
north. What these two features imply is hard to suggest, although it
is possible that the lake is also the result of quarrying.

The most interesting aspect of the site is on the spur to the north
of the motte. Here are two apparent ramparts, similar in some
respects to those found at the low lying Cymaron, except that here
there are also the remains of the foundations of a rectangular structure, possibly with ancillary buildings at its west end. The motte
and surrounding hills create a sheltered micro-climate, and although
it is possible that this is no more than a barn it may also have been
the 'llys' of the native Welsh dynasties of the twelfth century.
Certainly this is a major and extensive site. The lack of a bailey
ditch, the great height of this castle, and its similarity to other
contentious sites, all combine to suggest that this fortress was not
Norman.

Crug Eryr

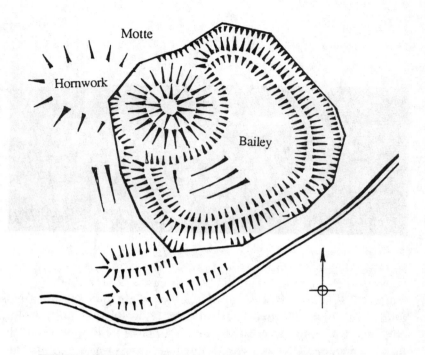

Motte

Hornwork

Bailey

Impressive motte and bailey in a lofty position
Location: 1.5km north-west of the junction of the A44
and A481 at Forest Inn (SO 158 593)
Access: Clearly visible from the A44

The castle may have been begun around 1150-60 by Cadwallon ap
Madog. It was probably taken around 1195 by the invading
Marchers. The castle was still occupied in the fourteenth century
when the descendants of the princes of Maelienydd lived there
composing bardic works. The castle was 'defaced' by Glyn Dwr in
the early fifteenth century.

There are several reasons to suggest that Crug Eryr was not a
Braose fortress, the most obvious being that it is a rather weak
motte and bailey castle built on a very substantial hill, not

commanding a stream or river crossing. The Normans were simply not overly inclined to build this type of castle at an altitude of 380 metres. The Welsh, however, appreciated height for their fortifications. Crug Eryr is a small motte and bailey with no real trace of a counterscarp bank around the motte's unprotected side, although there is a trace of a hornwork, which is surprising as there is no higher ground in this direction. To the eastern (English) side the rampart is far more powerful as though this was a 'show castle' to impress those arriving from this direction! The curiously shaped bailey—it is best described as roughly rectangular, though the plan might suggest that it has been altered at a later date, possibly with the addition of the motte or tower—has no real trace of an entrance, except for the causeway to the south which crosses the ditch. Recent damage to the site, especially to the north and south angles, has revealed that the rampart consists of tightly packed shale fragments, which possibly marks the core of a rubble curtain wall. Certainly this rubble appears to cross the motte ditch. To the south of the bailey are two slight mounds which may have been connected with the entrance. The pasture below the site to the south may at some time have been levelled as an outer enclosure, for certainly the present remains are of no great size or strength.

Towards the dingle north-east of the site are a series of curious apparently non–defensive banks and ditches, which may have been for show, or perhaps something to do with the spring which apparently rose at the top of this series of structures. An excavation in the 1930s uncovered walls and Norman doorways, but unfortunately the excavation was never written up and the photographs are apparently now lost.

Crug Eryr was apparently one of the few minor castles occupied after the Norman era in the Middle March. Despite this it does not appear in the 1304, survey, the most detailed of those for the Mortimer lands in Radnor Barony. This may indicate that it was in Welshry, the district populated by the Welsh, as was Knighton, Norton and Pilleth, which were also not described in any detail. The unmentioned nearby vill of Llanfihangel Nant Melan was also apparently in Welshry. Llanfihangel certainly existed before 1230, and most likely before 1211, when it was held by Meurig ab Ieuaf and William Braose. Tradition has it that Einion Sais ap Hywel ap Gruffydd ap Goronwy ap Gwrgenau ap Hoeddlyw ap Cadwgan ab Elystan lived at Tomen Krygeryr, and held the land on both sides of it. By the mid-fifteenth century the castle had apparently been abandoned when a mansion to replace it was commenced in the lowlands below at Harpton. One seventeenth century source speaks of it having been 'defaced' by Glyn Dwr. The historical lament to Cadwallon ap Madog also suggests that his power spread into this district. In a long and difficult poem he is credited with being 'chief lord over Gwernarglwydd' or Cefnyraelwyd and 'the renowned possessor of Clud'. That Cadwallon was mentioned in this area may well suggest that Castell Crug Eryr was built by, or for him, in the mid-twelfth century, as it certainly appears to have been in land then under his influence. It could also have been constructed as a convenient spring board for Cadwallon's continuing ambitions in Elfael, at the junction of the routes between Radnor, Elfael Uwch Mynydd and Maelienydd, which even today are important routeways.

Tomen Castle

A large motte on a spur
Location: 0.5km north of the junction of the A44
and A481 at Forest Inn (SO 172 589)
Access: On private land, can be seen from the A44

This castle, lying 340 metres above sea level, was possibly a Braose outpost in the Welshry of Radnor and held by their allies, a minor branch of the dynasty of Maelienydd. This can be deduced by a charter made during the rule of a William Braose probably in the later part of the period 1140 to 1208. By this document, that only survives as a meagre confirmation of 1231, William Braose and Meurig ab Ade granted the church of St Michael in 'Nantmelan' to St Davids. The joint grant would seem to indicate that William Braose was the overlord of Meurig, whilst the rights in the church would most likely belong to the holder of the nearby castle.

In the summer of 1211 King John waged a short, sharp war against Llywelyn ab Iorwerth which forced him to surrender by 15 August. Apparently three members of the dynasty of Maelienydd, who had been prominent in their opposition to the king, surrendered with him. Their opposition to the Crown can be judged by the weight of the fines they each bore as part of the peace negotiations. Madog ap Maelgwn (ap Cadwallon ap Madog) was fined £100 26s. 8d. to obtain the king's goodwill, and Meurig ab Ade and Philip ap Rhys were fined 100 marks each. The identification of this Philip ap Rhys is somewhat problematical, but most likely he was someone of only local importance. Meurig ab Ade's identification is also problematical. Considering this Meurig's apparent rebellion in favour of William Braose in Wales between 1209 and 1211, it is possible that he is also known as Meurig ab Ieuaf of Llanfihangel-nant-Melan who appears in many genealogies of the princes of Maelienydd. If this is one and the same person, then Meurig's gene-alogical father Ieuaf, or Ade, of Cefnllys, might be the same as the 'Ade Bidebach' who brought troops, probably from the Herefordshire March, to London in 1185 to help Henry II in his continental wars. It therefore seems possible that here, as elsewhere in the March, we have junior members of the dynasty of Maelienydd in the service of the Marchers and probably in opposition to their cousins, the chief lords of Maelienydd. The same thing happened elsewhere in the March, for example in Powys, where the family of Iorwerth Goch, a lord who was often, if not always, in the pay of the Crown, was gradually squeezed out of the principality, eventually settling in Sutton in Shropshire. From there they were to solidly support their king in the vain hope of one day regaining their lost territories in Wales.

The next year, 1212, Madog ap Maelgwn and Meurig ab Ieuaf jointly paid £168 to the sheriff of Hereford, who acknowledged receipt of the sum. Apparently this accounted for the entire fine as it is not mentioned again. Payment was probably made before the month of May, for a general war then once again broke out between many Welsh princes and King John. John was forced to return to the Marches and relieve his followers who were closely besieged in their castles. On the royal relief of Mathrafal Castle in Montgomeryshire, the first action of its lord, Robert Vipont, had been to hang his seven year old hostage, Rhys ap Maelgwn, at Shrewsbury. King John soon followed suit, hanging the rebellious Hywel ap Cadwallon, Madog ap Maelgwn and Meurig Barach, possibly the last lord of Tomen Castle, at Bridgnorth on his way back to Nottingham. They were supposedly hanged for the killing of one William Moid, but more likely for open rebellion. In the Welsh chronicles the three are recorded as 'eminent men of the lineage of princes', 'leaders of gentle birth', or 'venerable men'— the days of the princes of Maelienydd were already seen as over. It is possible that Meurig Barach's castle was destroyed at around the same time.

Knighton

A motte and bailey heavily built over
Location: On top of a rise in the centre of the town
(SO 284 722)
Access: On private land, next to the fire station

The castle was probably founded before 1086 by Hugh L'Asne and then inherited by the Chandos family. Roger Chandos rebelled against Henry II, only coming to terms with him in 1186 at Wrockwardine in Shropshire. Knighton and Norton castles, however, seem to have been retained by the Crown, although Snodhill Castle in Herefordshire was returned. The two Radnorshire castles were apparently passed to royal officials. During the troubles of 1191, when Roger Mortimer was exiled by the Justiciar, William Braose of Radnor was paid 20 marks compensation for Knighton Castle which the government had probably taken from him. At the same time Walter Clifford and Hugh Say were recompensed £7 8s. for garrisoning Knighton and Norton castles. Roger Mortimer returned from exile on his French estates by 1194, by which time William Braose seems to have regained both castles. In March, 1207, King John demanded the castles back from Braose and transferred them to the custody of Roger Mortimer. On 12 June, 1207, Roger was ordered to pass Knighton and Norton with their appurtenances to Robert Sineford, the bailiff of Thomas Erdington the then sheriff of Shropshire. Mortimer obviously was not happy with his instructions and on 19 July, John again tersely ordered Roger to transfer Knighton Castle as he had been mandated to do. At the end of May, 1208, William Braose, in the course of a much wider campaign, unsuccessfully attacked both Knighton and Norton castles, but could not dislodge Thomas Erdington from them. Thomas remained in possession of both castles, the escheat of Roger Chandos as they were called in 1211, until May 1215 when Llywelyn ab Iorwerth in alliance with the remains of the Braose clan stormed both castles and destroyed them.

In reply to this act, Hugh Mortimer of Wigmore made an agreement with Thomas Erdington swapping the two castles for land in

Hampshire. He then tried, by legal means, to regain the land from the prince of Gwynedd. Llywelyn, who was now in seisin, would have none of it and wrote scornfully to the regency complaining of Hugh's legal chicanery. With this, the matter was allowed to rest until 1230 when Hugh Mortimer's brother and legal heir, Ralph, a fifty year old bachelor, married Llywelyn's daughter and saved the Mortimer clan of Wigmore from extinction by siring two sons with her. As a dower Llywelyn granted the newly-weds Knighton and Norton, so finally placing them back in the hands of the Mortimers. It is to be presumed that Ralph was then responsible for rebuilding both castles, which are known to have been masonry structures.

Knighton town was granted murage in 1260 after its destruction by the Welsh of Ceri on 23 April of that year. Despite this, Knighton and Norton castles surrendered to Owain ap Madog in 1262 when they were finally destroyed.

Standing in the centre of the town, little actually remains of Knighton Castle. What does remain of this motte and bailey has been badly encroached upon by the buildings that surround and lie upon it. The motte is towards the west side and has been badly damaged by the fire station built into that side of the site. The bailey seems to be oval and is similarly disfigured.

Bryn y Castell

A large ditched motte
Location: At the east end of Knighton (SO 290 722)
Access: It lies above the car park at the east end of the town

The history of Knighton Castle is further confused by the motte and possible bailey at Bryn y Castell just east of the town. Its position is most curious, being less than a mile east of the main castle. It would seem unlikely that both sites were founded by the Chandos family in the twelfth century. Probably it is best to date this castle to after 1215 when Llywelyn ab Iorwerth seized Knighton and Norton for his principality. Bryn y Castell could therefore be seen as the Marcher reaction to this threat to Wigmore. It is known that other Marchers had empowered Brian Brampton of Brampton Bryan Castle to defend the valley of the Teme after the disasters of 1215 and it is therefore possible that this castle was built by him in the first half of the thirteenth century. The castle itself consists of a large circular motte with a deep ditch set on the edge of a large plateau above the River Teme and overlooking the town. It is certainly in a position to dominate the town. There is some rubble on the slopes of the motte and it is possible that it originally carried a shell keep. A bailey may have lain under the present sports pitch to the south of the motte. The castle was probably abandoned by 1231 after Ralph Mortimer had obtained title to Knighton and had begun rebuilding the slighted defences. (See also Knighton above.)

Norton

A damaged motte
Location: On the west side of the B4355, near the road's
summit at the northern end of the village (SO 303 673)
Access: Is visible from the B4355

A 7.5m high motte set in the garden of a modern house, over-looking a fall of ground to the north. There was a ditch around the tall conical motte, but there is no trace of masonry. The bailey has been built over, but its plan can still be made out in the boundaries of the gardens that have superseded it.

The history of the castle is largely identical to that of Knighton, for which see above.

Bleddfa

A large mound with slight remains of a square keep
Location: On the eastern edge of the village, north of the A488
Access: On private land, but visible from the A488

The castle was probably founded before 1100 by the lords of Richard's Castle who later held the barony and were in possession of the surrounding lands in 1086. The castle was overwhelmed at some point in the twelfth century and consequently, along with Cymaron and Painscastle, had to be rebuilt in 1195. In aid of this task Hugh Say of Richard's Castle was granted £5 by the Crown. The castle was next mentioned in November, 1262, when, along with Cefnllys, it was captured and destroyed by the men of Maelienydd. In 1304, the dowager lady of Richard's Castle obtained the king's permission to use the remains of the castle as a quarry to help build the tower of Bleddfa Church. This tower too has subsequently collapsed, but its foundations can still be seen adjoining the church.

Bleddfa consists of a tall motte in excess of 9m high. It is surrounded by a ditch and the remains of a counterscarp rampart which has been damaged by later tanning activities at the site. The slight traces of facing stone on the south-western side of the motte suggest that this is all that remains of a rectangular tower-keep that has largely collapsed in on itself, adding an extra 3m or so in height to the motte. The bailey to the north has been largely ploughed out, although it appears to have been roughly rectangular, and apparently has tower platforms towards both the east and west angles. Entrance to the site appears to have been from the east where a modern farm track now enters the site. To the south are traces of waterworks which, if early medieval in date, would have flooded this part of the valley and given the castle a lake to the west and south to add to its defence. In total this would have made a formidable little castle.

Pilleth: Castell Foelallt

A conical motte and remains of outer enclosures
Location: By the River Lugg south of Pilleth (SO 259 676)
Access: A bridleway leads past the site to its west.
It is also visible from the B4356

The castle was probably begun by Ralph Mortimer of Wigmore before 1086 when the surrounding districts were recorded as being held by him. Nothing else of certainty was recorded of the castle until 1341, when it was described as the residence of a dowager lady of Wigmore. Surprisingly, it does not seem to have played any part in the battle of Pilleth in 1402.

Pilleth has a small steep-sided motte some 7.5m high. It is surrounded by a ditch that has a counterscarp on the exposed south and east, but no rampart on the bailey side. Rubble around the motte top and in the ditch combined with the shape of the motte tends to suggest that a tower once stood here. The bailey is exceptionally small and only has a rampart on its most exposed north-western side. The entrance may have been gained through a break in this rampart, though this feature may well be modern. Little now remains of the outer ward, although a slightly sunken path shows what was probably the main route from the motte, through both baileys, to what must have been an entrance to the site at the north-western apex of the outer ward. The irregular mound which over-looks this entrance consists of natural gravels, and almost certainly predates the outer enclosure, as seen by the way the sunken path skirts around it. On the north-eastern side, the inner bailey rampart has been continued down to a small stream, apparently forming a small triangular enclosure, although this area is overlooked by the scarp in the next field. It is possible that this field marks the site of a main ward, or possibly even a village enclosure.

Presteign

Looking over the bailey towards the motte

Low mounds of the bailey and motte remain
Location: In Presteign's park at the north-western edge
of the town (SO 310 645)
Access: By footpaths in the park

The castle itself may have been begun by the lords of Richard's
Castle before Domesday by which time Presteign was already a
valuable settlement. Presteign seems to have been first mentioned
in the survey as *Humet*, meaning a meadow on a boundary. Later
this was changed to Priests'-*humet* to distinguish it from nearby
Kinsham (*Kingeshemede* in 1216) which was the king's share of the
humet. The Domesday Survey states that in Leintwardine Hundred,
Osbern fitz Richard held Presteign (*Humet*) which he had held from
King Edward the Confessor in his time (1042-1066). Here there
were two men at arms with 1 plough, 5 villagers, 5 smallholders
and 1 radman with 3 ploughs between them. There was land here
for 20 ploughs, but it was all waste both before the Conquest and at
1086, except for the lordship itself which was valued at 10 shil-

lings. This may suggest that Presteign Castle was operational by then. Surrounding Presteign were the vills of Stanage, Cascob and Ackhill (*Achel*) all of which belonged to the lords of Richard's Castle. In 1137-9 *Prestehemed* belonged to Osbern's grandson, Osbern fitz Hugh of Richard's Castle. Sometime after this, Presteign Castle passed to Roger Port of Kington and Osbern built a new castle as the centre of this part of the barony at nearby Stapleton, which now lies just inside Herefordshire. However, he failed in his probable objective of retaking Presteign during the anarchy of Stephen's reign.

During the Ports' control of Presteign, which lasted until their banishment in 1172, they seem to have established the Fraxino family as lords of Presteign Castle. After 1172, the Ports' barony of Kington seems to have virtually become an appendage of the sheriffdom of Hereford, until in 1203 William Braose of Radnor bought the barony and therefore Presteign. On William's rebellion in 1208, Thomas Fraxino seems to have successfully withdrawn his lands around Presteign into a barony he held directly from King John. However, on Braose's return to royal fealty in 1218 he again found himself subject to the barony of Kington. In 1230, the land and castle of Presteign passed to Ralph Mortimer as custodian of the Braose lands. Later he married his son and heir Roger to Maud Braose, an heiress of the last William Braose and through her the Mortimers gained overlordship of the Fraxinos of Presteign. In 1244, Thomas Fraxino made a charter in favour of Wigmore Abbey in the hall of his castle. Eighteen years later the castle was captured and destroyed by Llywelyn's forces. As a consequence, in 1337 it was recorded as merely 'a plot of land called Castle Ditch'. This hardly suggests that it was still defensible.

The castle now consists of an oval ringwork roughly 12 metres north-south by 24 metres east-west. Entrance was gained from a similar sized and shaped bailey to the east. The only ditching at the site is to the west where the ringwork is protected by a trench cut across the neck of the hill. The bailey to the east has been mutilated by more recent landscaping.

Discoed

A small mound
Location: In front of the church (SO 277 648)
Access: From the lane by the church

Although the vill was mentioned in the Domesday Book there seems to have been little effort to fortify this area. The small mound in front of the church may be an aborted attempt at a castle foundation.

Stanage

A small motte and bailey
Location: West of Stanage Park (SO 331 731)
Access: Can be seen from the main road

Just west of Stanage Park lie the remains of a small motte and bailey castle. The motte is heavily damaged but still about 7m high. The denuded, roughly triangular bailey platform is to the east. Although large fragments of stream-washed rubble and gravel litters the site, no trace of masonry could be found.

The vill of Stanage was held of the Says of Richard's Castle and the castle here may well have been abandoned by 1215 when this district was transferred to the control of Brian Brampton in an attempt to stop the Welsh penetrating further down the Teme valley. (See Knighton, above, for additional information.)

Rhaeadr–Gwy

A much mutilated motte
Location: To the west of the Wye at Rhayader (SN 967 678)
Access: Can be seen from the road to the Elan Valley,
near the church, but the motte has a garage built into it
and the bailey is covered by private gardens

The castle was founded in 1177 by Rhys ap Gruffydd, prince of Deheubarth, soon after the death of Einion Clud of Elfael, traditionally around Christmas 1176. The castle was fully operational by 1184 when Rhys ap Gruffydd made a charter at the church of Saint Bridget at 'Raiadr'. By this document Rhys, in the presence of his army, granted the grange of Cwmwd Deuddwr, or Elenydd, surrounding his castle, except for the land on the west bank of the Wye, to Strata Florida Abbey. As the church of Saint Bridget and the land of the castle were both on the west bank of the Wye, this goes to confirm that this site was Rhys' castle of Rhaeadr-gwy, rather than the later Mortimer site on the opposite bank (SN 969 681). The castle was probably destroyed around 1190 by the princes of Maelienydd who were infuriated by Rhys' incursion onto what they regarded as their land. Giraldus claims that the castle was miraculously burned down as the garrison had mischievously stolen a religious relic. However, the Welsh chronicles consistently name the real culprits! Rhys tried to re-assert his authority in the region in 1194, but once more Maelgwn and Hywel ap Cadwallon seized his castle and burned it. The castle seems to have been left a ruin after this, although in the Civil War of 1642-46 the ruins of the tower on the motte are said to have been forced into use, housing a gun battery.

Little now remains, though in 1982 enough remained to suggest that the motte had a revetment, and possibly a stone tower, for foundations of such a structure could still be seen on the top of the motte in the eighteenth century, when it was known as Tower Hill. It is uncertain whether the current slight masonry remains on the motte are original, but if they are they may mark the remnants of a round tower, of a kind apparently favoured by Rhys ap Gruffydd. The bailey would appear to have been roughly rectangular, and was apparently not walled.

Rhaeadr

A rock cut ditch partially enclosing a roughly triangular area
Location: South of the church in Rhayader (SN 968 680)
Access: Part of a public playground

The castle may have been begun around 1200 as the Mortimer replacement of the old princely castle of Rhaeadr-gwy. The local Welsh seem to have besieged the castle and after a two week operation forced the garrison to leave, allowing them to keep their lives and 'their members intact'! Roger Mortimer, on hearing of the siege, rushed back from Normandy where he was aiding King John, but was too late to affect the outcome.

The buildings were described as merely the 'site of an old castle' in 1307 and 1424, yet in an indenture of 1316 it was mentioned as a castle. Probably, as a legal conveyance, this was merely a formality for a long destroyed fortress. In 1783, a mass grave was opened in the churchyard just north of the castle site. The opinion of the day was that these allegedly beheaded skeletons were the remains of Mortimer's garrison, even though they were supposed to have been allowed to leave unhindered. More likely they were the remains of criminals or casualties of the bloody wars that repeatedly ruined the land of Gwrtheyrnion during the darker times of the Middle Ages.

Cwm y Saeson (or Dulas)

Low-lying earthworks at a junction of streams
Location: 9km north of Rhayader (SN 961 771)
Access: Visible from the road to its north

The site of Dulas 'Castle', set in a wide marsh, consists of a small, approximately 6m by 9m, rectangular ringwork, protected to the north, south and east by streams, and on the exposed west by a shallow moat, additionally protected by a ditch and rampart. This latter part of the fortification is remarkably similar to that at Cymaron, and it is possible that both these additional defences were the work of Roger Mortimer in the early thirteenth century. The entrance to the ringwork was to the north, and slightly inturned. The causeway to the west, which approaches the site, over what would probably have been marsh, may suggest a prehistoric origin, but the name of the area, Cwm y Saeson (Valley of the English), would certainly infer an English, and therefore probably Mortimer influence. So too would the fact that the site is at the north-western extremity of Roger Mortimer's 1200 grant to Cwmhir.

Glan Edw (Brynllwyd Mount)

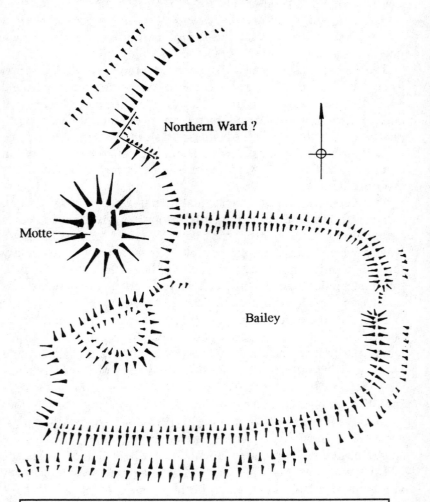

Northern Ward ?

Motte

Bailey

Impressive castle mound with large baileys
Location: 0.5km south-east of Hundred House (SO 116 543)
Access: On private land, but can be seen from the A481

The castle is the only motte and bailey in the commote of Elfael Uwch Mynydd. It commands the crossing of the Edw and was probably the original Colwyn Castle for the simple reason that it is a low lying massive motte and bailey. It follows that the present day Colwyn Castle is the successor to the valley site.

The castle was probably commenced around 1093 by Ralph Tosny of Clifford, taken by the forces of Madog ab Idnerth around 1135 and then rebuilt by Hugh Mortimer of Wigmore in 1144. It was not mentioned again and must have reverted to Welsh control, probably with the defeat of Hugh by his Angevin enemies in the period 1148-53. The castle was rebuilt by the forces of William Braose in 1195 and besieged and finally destroyed by Prince Rhys ap Gruffydd in 1196.

The castle consists of a substantial motte, some 10.5m in height, which was surrounded by a moat fed from the Edw, whose course has now moved away from the site. The ground about the castle was very marshy and the platform of the main ward was apparently formed by piling up gravel from the river bed. On the three sides of this rectangular bailey with its rounded corners, a rampart was thrown up for added protection. This rampart contains many large stones, but there is no definitive evidence of a curtain wall, although the extent of masonry in the motte ditch and on the bailey facing the mound indicates the possibility. There are also strong indications of walling at the north-western apex of the site, apparently beyond the main castle defences. However, this may be a spoil heap cleared from the motte ditch, later buildings, or a further ward to the north of which nothing else remains. The possible presence of a ward here is further strengthened by the ditch to the southern ward not continuing around the northern side of the site.

The entrance was possibly gained from the northern side, perhaps via the northern ward, at a kink in the rampart which would have been overshadowed by the motte. The present entrance and the filling of the ditch to the east is almost certainly modern. The access to the motte is also problematical, for there are two possibilities. First there is a definite lowering of the platform into the motte ditch at roughly its midpoint opposite the motte, whilst next to this is a raised semi-circular platform with slight traces of walling around its summit; walls which still existed in the nineteenth century. This may have been a forebuilding to the motte, or possibly even a relatively modern non-defensive structure. Whichever it was it leads to the most interesting feature of this substantial site.

One of the first things to strike the eye about Glan Edw is the strange shape of the motte. The south-eastern face slumps quite dramatically into the ditch. Close examination of the masonry-strewn slope reveals that the motte on this side is far less compact, and gives a firm impression of an apparent motte slighting. (This also occurs at the northern English castles of Groby, Dunham Massey, Kirby Malzeard, Northallerton, Thirsk and Weston Turville.) It is tempting to equate this slumping with the destruction of the castle by Rhys ap Gruffydd in 1196, but it must be remembered that it was not uncommon for mottes to be unable to carry the weight of stone towers built upon them. What is certain is that any such collapse is unlikely to predate 1196, although it is likely that the castle had only been recovered by Braose forces some twelve months before this. However, much of this slumping may be due to quarrying, which was apparently occurring here around the turn of the century. On the motte top are substantial traces of two straight walls running roughly north-south. They seems to be best interpreted as the remains of an elongated tower or shell keep measuring some 18m by 7.5m externally. Such an unusual structure would probably be best dated to the twelfth century.

Penarth and Fforest Wood, two surrounding castles

> A prominent mound
> Location: 2km south-east of Hundred House (SO 124 526)
> Access: Lies west of the road from Colwyn Castle to Aberedw

> An intermediate sized motte
> Location: 2km south-west of Hundred House (SO 101 529)
> Access: In private woodland

When the lordship of Colwyn was initiated, probably in 1093, Ralph Tosny, the founder, probably granted lands around his major castle to knights in return for feudal duties. Sites of two of their castles are traceable. Little remains at Penarth but for the steep-sided and possibly natural conical motte which has been artificially steepened, and which overlooks a sharp fall in ground to the south. Surprisingly there is no trace of a bailey although there is room for one to the north. The ditch is shallow and uneven as if parts of it were considered too difficult to cut. In a similar position to its companion to the east, Fforest motte is apparently a totally man-made structure, some 4.5m high and well ditched, as its closeness to the hillside would demand. There is no trace of any bailey. It is possible that the motte at Aberedw is part of this group, though it was later to form a separate lordship. The castles' history would probably have been the same as that of Glan Edw above.

Guanceste

A flattened mound and platforms
Location: On Guanceste Hill, 2km south-west of
Forest Inn (SO 156 569)
Access: Public paths lead past the mound

Guanceste is a possible castle site on the Elfael/Llythyfnwg border which would have blocked a high pass into central Rhwng Gwy a Hafren from the lowlands of Radnor lordship. The remains are now heavily denuded, but appear to have been a small, now badly collapsed, motte, with two roughly triangular platforms—apparently artificially levelled and which appear to have been baileys—one to the north, and one to the south. There are no traces of any ditches, or bailey ramparts, but the absence of these is possibly due to the poor condition of the site. The remains are overlooked by nearby higher ground, upon which the 'castle' could have been built with little further effort. Many prehistoric sites litter the surrounding countryside.

Colwyn

Extent of
Roman fort

A481

Castle ringwork set inside an earlier Roman fort
Location: 1km south-west of Hundred House (SO 108 540)
Access: Visible from the A481

As has been noted under Glan Edw, it would seem unlikely that the castle now known as Colwyn was actually founded much before 1196 when its predecessor was abandoned. The fortress was probably begun around 1200 when William Braose was granted rights of conquest in this district. It was probably taken from him on his rebellion in 1208. On his sons' subsequent rebellion in 1215, Colwyn was one of King John's castles which were left for Gwallter ab Einion Clud to take on behalf of his Braose allies. The castle seems to have remained in Welsh hands throughout the rule of Llywelyn ab Iorwerth, the truce brokers from England and Wales meeting there to discuss the state of the border in 1232. On Llywelyn's death the local princes seem to have managed to transfer their allegiance easily to that of Henry III and to have remained in possession of the castle site. They paid their homage to Henry on 3 February, 1241. It is quite possible that the castle was, at this time, regarded as an appurtenance of Builth Wells which was granted to Llywelyn by its Braose lord in 1229. The cantref of Buellt had been seized by Henry III in 1240 and the castle there refortified by John of Monmouth.

In 1248, Sir Owain ap Maredudd ab Einion Clud was recorded as holding all Elfael Uwch Mynydd, and therefore by implication Colwyn Castle, when it was unsuccessfully claimed from him by his cousin Roger Vaughan ab Gwallter Clud. In July 1260, Sir Owain, by then a sub-tenant of Roger Mortimer, surrendered to Prince Llywelyn after the fall of Builth Wells Castle. Sir Owain seems to have weathered the following storms and in 1276/7 successfully returned to royal allegiance with the support of his many, now fully grown, sons. However, the old Sir Owain and his sons rose in favour of Llywelyn immediately before his death on 11 December, 1282, and as a consequence they lost Colwyn Castle and the lands of their ancestors in Elfael. The castle then passed into the hands of, and was possibly rebuilt by, Maud Mortimer (d.1303), the widow of Roger (d.1282). The fortress was mentioned in 1309 and in 1337, but seems to have been abandoned by 1397 when the Beauchamps were ruling Elfael from their base at Painscastle. It is indicative that no mention of its use seems to have been made during the Glyn Dwr rebellion.

Colwyn Castle consists of a raised circular ringwork, set on a rise above the River Edw on the site of a Roman fort. It was a stone castle, but later buildings on the site have obscured all certain trace of this, although thirteenth century mouldings remain visible in the farm walls. The earthworks would appear to place it in a class of the thirteenth century hill castles like Diserth and the late Mortimer castles. It is possible that the well preserved Roman defences were reused as a large outer enclosure or even town defences judging by their size.

Painscastle

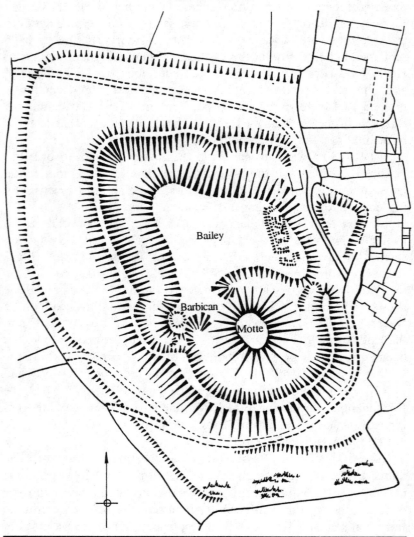

Bailey

Barbican

Motte

Motte, bailey and deep ditches
Location: At the south-western corner of Painscastle (SO 166 462)
Access: On private land, but partly visible from the B4594

Painscastle is probably named after its builder, Pain fitz John. Consequently, it is unlikely to have been built much before 1120. Pain was killed in July 1137 and the castle probably fell to the forces of Madog ab Idnerth soon afterwards. It may have been rebuilt by the lord of Ewias Harold in 1140 and destroyed again soon afterwards. The site then seems to have remained in native hands until the great Marcher assault of 1195 when Maud Braose is credited with slaughtering the Welsh at Painscastle. The following year Prince Rhys of Deheubarth attacked the castle and seized the land around it. However, before the castle could be brought to terms Rhys agreed to a truce with William Braose who was attacking Rhys' ancestral lands in Ceredigion to the west. In 1198, Prince Gwenwynwyn of Powys led the remaining princes of central Wales in a foolhardy and ill-starred attack on the castle. The castle was taken from William Braose by the king in 1208, but re-taken by Gwallter ab Einion Clud in 1215 with the Braoses' sanction. In August 1216, Gwallter made his peace with King John and briefly became the prince of all Elfael, although it is doubtful that John recognized him as anything more than an expedient ally. The castle was probably destroyed soon afterwards when Llywelyn received the homage of the Welsh of Elfael, possibly after Gwallter Clud's death which occurred after 1220. Llywelyn's grasp on Painscastle was no doubt augmented by the capture of William Braose in 1228, when Llywelyn's man, who was probably Roger Vaughan ap Gwallter Clud, was campaigning in the territory. The castle site was retaken and refortified in good quality stonework by Henry III in 1231. The castle and its buildings were then regularly mentioned down to 1255 when it was re-granted to Roger Tosny, the descendant of its earlier Tosny lords. Roger died young in 1264, and in 1265 the castle was taken and destroyed by Llywelyn. Twelve years later it was rebuilt by Ralph Tosny, and was still defensible in 1401 when it was garrisoned against Owain Glyn Dwr.

Today the main feature of the castle is the large motte. Traces of foundations suggest that it originally supported a round tower, though the foundations have largely been grubbed up. Entrance to the keep was apparently gained through a barbican which crossed the motte ditch to the west. In 1231, £72 was spent on this barbican and the provision of a drawbridge. The bailey is roughly rectangular and deeply ditched, with a strong counterscarp bank. It too shows evidence of the stone walls having been grubbed up, robber trenches running around the lip of the ward. The overall shape of the castle is that of a playing card, and as a Roman fort could be expected in this area it is possible that this is what was originally here. Indeed, Roman pavements have been found at the site.

Dolbedwyn and Llandeilo Graben, two surrounding castles

A damaged motte
Location: 2km south-west of Newchurch (SO 205 491)
Access: Visible to the east from the road that links the
B4594 to the south-west of Newchurch with Clyro

A medium sized motte
Location: 3km east of Llandeilo Graben (SO 125 449)
Access: On private land, but visible from a field gate near
the road junction to the west

Just as Colwyn appears to have had knightly castles protecting it so too does Painscastle. Flanking the site to the east and west are two mottes. That to the east and visible from Painscastle is Dolbedwyn, which like Penarth to the north, may be a scarped natural mound. It is set in the confluence of two streams and commands access to the Arrow valley and England. Apparently this mound, roughly a mile north of Rhosgoch, was known as Llys Ifor, which may suggest as a possible occupier either the father of Hywel ab Ifor, or more likely Ifor ap Gruffydd who held lands in this district in the late thirteenth century. This approximately 6m high motte had a deep ditch and rampart, but no bailey, although one may have been planned to the west towards the road. The site has been much damaged by rabbits this century and now bears little resemblance to a castle motte.

Its companion motte, situated on a spur above the Bach Howey in the parish of Llandeilo Graben does not seem to have a bailey either. This mound, much larger than the other surrounding castle sites mentioned, appears to be totally man-made, and has the greatest area of platform on the motte top, some twenty-five feet in diameter. It is also some 7.5m high from the bottom of the ditch. This motte was undoubtedly built to support a palisade (or curtain of which some foundations appear to remain buried) around a tower or hall. The narrowness of the other motte surfaces, except perhaps for Fforest, something less than 6m across, indicates that these were meant for towers alone.

Cwrt Evan Gwynne

A medium sized motte
Location: 1km north of Clyro (SO 215 448)
Access: Can be seen from the road

This castle may be the work of Cadwallon ap Madog; certainly its plan and position seem to suggest this. It is set in a hollow, some way below the summit of the high hills above the Wye, between a small stream and a probable Roman road which ran from Clyro to Painscastle. The motte is comparable to others possibly built by Cadwallon, and may have only had a ditch between it and the now built over bailey. The bailey was apparently rectangular and may have led to another much larger one to the south, though this is now difficult to judge as it has been disfigured by a farmhouse and its associated buildings. The bailey appears to have been ditched only towards the motte, where a possible causeway may have connected it to the keep, as at Buddugre. Apparently the castle was strongly fortified in stone, although there is now little trace of this. The shape of the motte suggests that a polygonal tower once stood upon it. The suggested Roman road appears to have taken a route superseded by the castle ditch on the west side of the site and then continues as a clearly visible footpath up the side of the hill.

Caemardy

A small motte
Location: 2km north of Builth Wells (SO 035 531)
Access: On private land

Castell Caemardy could be one of the more interesting of the small mottes, for it may have been one of the defensive measures taken by the princes of Elfael against their brethren of Maelienydd in the late twelfth century. This small 'motte' is the highest placed of all the Elfael mottes, although again it does not occupy the highest position available. It is only some 3m high and set uncomfortably above a steep scarp at the edge of a plain that was possibly once a pasture. Once more there is no bailey, but there is a slight trace of a ditch on the exposed side, which again shows a marked similarity to the other more curious Middle March sites. It is also possible that it could be a prehistoric burial mound, possibly converted to a motte.

Llowes

A medium sized motte
Location: 1km south of Llowes on the banks
of the Wye (SO 191 407)
Access: On private land, but can be seen from the
lay-by on the A438 to the south-west of Llowes

Little remains of Llowes Castle and in a few years even this may be gone. At present the motte stands precariously on the brink of the River Wye, which eats more and more into the site each year. In 1985, the maps show that the river was 150 yards south-west of Llowes Castle with a farm track running south of the boundary fence. In 1995, the river was virtually up to the base of the motte, with a consequence that the track and boundary had been partly washed away and another farm track had been created inside the actual field and north of the motte. Also washed away appears to have been the small square enclosure reported in the 1960s. Apparently the top of the motte was damaged by a military post during the Second World War. It appears to have been one of several sites that were fortified as part of the training for General Patton's American army before D-Day, and probably consisted of a bunker and field gun.

Clyro (La Royl)

A surprisingly large ringwork on a knoll
Location: Towards the southern edge of Clyro (SO 214 436)
Access: Can be seen to the east of the B4351 to Hay

The castle may have been begun in the 1070s as a companion to the main castle in nearby Hay-on-Wye. Together these two castles would have guarded the passage of the Wye. The castle was probably destroyed (or had been abandoned) by the 1140s. Certainly the lands round about the castle were granted to Abbey Cwmhir by the princes of Elfael sometime during the period 1176 to 1215. The castle was probably rebuilt after the Tosny family regained Elfael in 1276 and was still defensible in 1403.

Clyro is a peculiarly large castle. It is also unusual in that it was first mentioned in 1397 and there is no written evidence for the date of its foundation. The castle occupies the highest point of a now wooded knoll about a mile north of Hay-on-Wye Castle. On the summit is a large ringwork with a strong counterscarp bank around the base. A polygonal curtain wall once enclosed the site and a collapse on the western side shows that this wall had finely-cut quoins and may have been rebuilt at least once. Entrance was probably gained from the south where there may have been a gatehouse or keep. The lack of flanking towers in the curtain suggests an early date.

Glasbury

All but destroyed
Location: Near the centre of the village (SO 175 392)
Access: By the roads built partially on it!

This castle may have been started before 1088, although it is far more likely to have been begun in 1144 when the land was acquired from Gloucester monastery by the first Walter Clifford. It may have fallen and been retaken around 1165-75 when it was confirmed to its sub-tenant, Walter Clifford, who had ousted the Tosnys from their rights both in this vill and Clifford. When the last Walter Clifford rebelled in the late summer of 1233, the castle was surrendered to royal forces under Henry III and then garrisoned by Henry Turbeville. The castle was probably destroyed in the Welsh wars around 1265, for legal wrangles in the period 1274-80 do not mention it.

The castle has been effectively destroyed by developments in the 1960s. The very slight remains of the motte corresponds roughly to the present location of an access road into a cul-de-sac on the west side of Glasbury village. The western side of the site has been destroyed and built on already, while the eastern side has been removed in anticipation of future development. Its suggested position is now occupied by rough pasture and construction waste. It is clear that the ground levels were also reduced once the mound had been removed, probably to raise the ground levels elsewhere.

Twyn y Garth

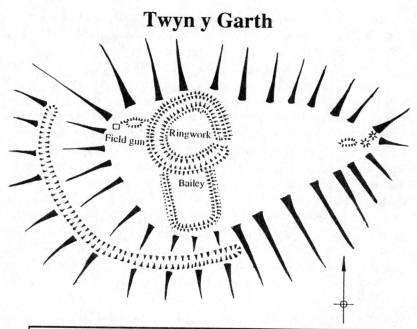

Field gun

Ringwork

Bailey

Weak ringwork and bailey with magnificent views
Location: 1.5km north-east of Erwood
Access: On common land reached by paths from a track
to the north of the hill on which it stands

The construction of this castle is probably best assigned to the
period 1208-10, and it was probably only occupied for a few years,
if at all, being abandoned by 1215. Even though it is most likely
that this castle dates to the thirteenth century when the Marchers
and even the king were building hill fortresses on a great scale
(including Cefnllys, Knucklas, Tinboeth, Degannwy and Dyserth) it
is possible that this is a Welsh castle. If this is the case then the
most likely builder would have been Einion Clud (k.1177) or his
brother, Cadwallon ap Madog (k.1179), both of whom were pre-
eminent in this region. A third possibility is that this site is thirteenth century Welsh, as Elfael and even Brycheiniog were repeatedly attacked and occasionally conquered by Venedotian invaders
(the inhabitants of Gwynedd) and their native allies throughout the

century. For example, a somewhat similar style of castle was apparently built by Maelgwn Fychan in 1242 at Llanilar (SN 630 746), assuming this is the Garth Grugyn referred to.

Indeed all that can be said of Twyn y Garth with certainty is that it is likely to have been commenced in the period 1070 to 1276 and that it was not long, if ever, garrisoned.

The climb up to Twyn y Garth affords spectacular views of the Wye valley as well as the surrounding amphitheatre of the mountains of Elfael and Brycheiniog. No doubt this was a primary reason for a castle being founded here and the castle defences may have encompassed the entire surface of this steep conical hill. Access to the site, then as now, is from the east, and commanding the track up from the valley are several features. The first is a small circular depression with a rubble-filled concave mound just beyond it. Some 61m to the west of these features, up a very slight slope, is the main castle ringwork. Between these two is a very slight trench, 15m long by 1.5m wide and approximately 0.5m deep. The purpose of this trench is uncertain, but as it has not been recorded in older surveys it seems reasonable to accept the view that this is part of the works known to have been undertaken by the Home Guard and General Patton's army during the Second World War.

It is noticeable that from the ringwork it is possible to view the base of the hill to the north and west whilst the view to the south and east is obscured by gently sloping ground. It therefore seems possible that the mound may have been a watchtower to control the dead ground to the east. If this was so, then the remnants would suggest that this was a small tower with walls some 1.5m thick and an internal diameter of 4.5m. Alternatively these features, and a similar 'raised depression' towards the eastern foot of the hill, directly under the 'cairns', may all be the remains of rifle pits of World War II vintage. Certainly, much military activity seems to have occurred in this district during the war years.

The main defences of the castle were undoubtedly the squashed oval ringwork of roughly 37m diameter set on the highest point of the hill. Entrance to this was apparently gained across a causeway passing over the ditch and breaking through the inner rampart beyond. The ditch is about 1.2m deep from the top of the rampart and appears to be virtually unchanged from its original depth.

External to the ditch is a slight 0.6m high counterscarp. On the inner side is a roughly 0.75m high rampart which protects the gently sloping south to north interior platform. There is no evidence of any internal buildings, but bedrock does protrude through the surface just north of the entrance. At the north-west 'corner' of the ring is a 0.75m deep pit of uncertain, but probably post-defensive use. It does not appear to be a well.

To the south of the ringwork lies a rectangular annex or bailey that covers the southern base of the hill in a similar manner to the suggested watchtower to the east. This bailey would have effectively doubled the internal area of the ringwork and is now only marked by a low 0.3m high rampart with the slightest trace of an accompanying external ditch. The large amounts of stone found in this slight bank may suggest that it was once a low wall or breastwork, although the flimsy nature of the entire site may suggest that the fortification was never completed and that what remains of the bailey is merely the marking out turfs and walls. Such works are not unknown and it is likely that all castles started out as a 'blueprint' on the ground, before construction proper was commenced. This may suggest that the castle, or at least the bailey, was never completed.

On the sloping platform between the ringwork and the slope proper is set an old World War I German field gun. This heavily rotted cannon is said to have been put in position between the wars and today still dominates the valley of the Wye, being plainly visible from miles around.

Between this gun and the ringwork counterscarp some 9m to the east are the foundations of what appears to be a small rectangular building, roughly 4.5m by 2.5m. Was this accommodation for the castle, or was it more to do with the suggested mining beneath the site? If the site is taken to include the ringwork and bailey it can be seen to cover all the approaches to the castle from the north, west and south. If the watch tower is included then the east is also fully covered giving the garrison an all round cover. This appears to be what was intended and as the entrance appears to have always been from the east these foundations west of the ringwork may well be traces of the original castle buildings, built outside the actual fortification, but under its protection. There may also have been slightly more protection from the elements for the garrison somewhat beneath the summit of the hill rather than right on top where the main fortifications were.

Aberedw I

A medium sized motte
Location: On the banks of the Edw in Aberedw (SO 078 472)
Access: By public footpath from the back of the church

The castle was possibly begun during the Marcher attacks on Wales during 1093 either by Ralph Tosny of Clifford or one of his Baskerville tenants. The castle was probably destroyed by 1150. It may have been rebuilt by the local Welsh princes, but it had certainly been destroyed by 1283. In 1284 the land of Aberedw was granted by Edmund Mortimer to his vassal Walter Hacklukel who built the new castle during 1284. However, the need for true castles had now passed and consequently Aberedw Castle, one of the last castles built in Wales, had been abandoned by 1397.

The motte at Aberedw, protects, as the name suggests, the entrance to the Edw valley. Ditched and ramparted on its most accessible side, it is built on the top of a steep scarp above the river and commanded the river plain before it. The castle shows the slightest traces of having an unditched, scarped bailey to the north, similar to that at Ceri in Montgomeryshire. On top of the motte lies a masonry filled horseshoe-shaped bank which marks the last remnants of a tower. Whether it was round, D–shaped or polygonal is now difficult to say, but certainly some of it has fallen into the river valley below due to erosion.

Aberedw II

Remains of round towers in a rectangular structure
Location: Adjacent to the old railway line (SO 076 474)
Access: A public path leads through the site from near the
road junction with the B4567, or continue on from Aberedw I

Walter Hacklukel started building a new square Edwardian castle
here, soon after the final dispossession of the last native lords of
this region, indicating that the motte predated this. The more
modern castle consists of a rectangular masonry enclosure that was
probably ditched all round. In the nineteenth century the railway
which passed underneath the site destroyed the western ditch and
used the castle remains as ballast. Round towers, now badly
damaged, stood at the four angles. The north-western tower appears
to have been larger than the other three. Perhaps this was a keep.
Entrance to the castle seems to have been gained from the flat
ground to the east.

Boughrood and Trewern

A damaged motte
Location: In the grounds of Boughrood House (SO 132 391)
Access: On private land, just visible from the road

A river headland isolated by a rock cut ditch
Location: On the southern bank of the Bach Howey (SO 121 435)
Access: Allegedly by public footpath, but all overgrown

Boughrood may have been begun by the Tosnys or Gamages around 1093. Like many of the Norman castles in this area it was probably taken and destroyed around 1150 and rebuilt about 1195. In 1205, the castle was seized from Matthew Gamages when he adhered to the French king in Normandy. On 11 July, the castle was transferred into the hands of Walter Clifford. On 7 December, 1206, the castle was again transferred, this time to the custody of the virtually dispossessed Roger Tosny. Roger died in 1209, but it is not known what happened to the castle. Probably, like the Elfael castles, it is likely that Boughrood changed hands in 1215, possibly being destroyed at this time. Certainly in March 1218, when Boughrood was re-granted to William Gamages in the peace settlement that followed the death of King John in 1216, only the land was mentioned and no castle. During the 1220s and 1230s the lordship was often a meeting point for commissions of truce between the English and Welsh, being on the boundary between Llywelyn's seisin (Colwyn and Aberedw) and the king's (Painscastle). Llywelyn, however, succeeded in annexing Boughrood during the wars of 1231-33. After Llywelyn's death Boughrood was retaken by the Gamages before 1242. William, the last Gamages, left the castle to his son-in-law Henry Pembridge who, during the war of 1257-60 commanded the king's army based on Monmouth. In the aftermath of the Treaty of Pipton, Boughrood fell to Llywelyn's forces and the castle was destroyed. In 1278, Henry Pembridge regained the land from his princely opponent, Rhys ap Roger Vaughan. The castle, despite being often mentioned in legal proceedings for the next 20 years, was probably never rebuilt.

Trewern Castle was first mentioned in these court cases from 1278 onwards. It too was probably never rebuilt. Consequently, it may have been built to protect the hinterland of Boughrood in the 1220s or 40s and became uneconomic to reconstruct after peace was achieved with Llywelyn in 1277.

There is little left of the motte at Boughrood because farm buildings have very much encroached upon it. The summit of the low mound appears to be enclosed by a bank which may be the remains of a masonry tower but seems more likely to be the soil tip of the 1960s excavators, who failed to find any trace of masonry on the motte, but did uncover much late domestic material. All trace of the bailey has disappeared under the farm which probably developed out of the castle. The name appears to be an Anglicization of 'Bach-rhyd' meaning 'little ford'.

Extensive earthworks north-west of the church and between it and Boughrood Court may be the remains of a shrunken village.

Trewern Castle is set at a primary bend of a stream which has been isolated by a rock cut ditch 3.5m deep and 12m in width across the southern end. The summit has an area of 27m by 9m tapering southwards to only 3.5m where the entrance must have been. Precipitous tree-covered slopes fall to the River Howey on the north, east and west sides. Apart from the ditch no evidence of human workmanship in any form can be seen, but this is not unusual in a site only briefly occupied.

Recent books from Logaston Press

Owain Glyn Dwr
The War of Independence in the Welsh borders

by Geoffrey Hodges, this book concentrates on the background to and the actual fighting in the borders. The tensions leading up to the revolt are considered, as are the politics of early fifteenth century England and Wales. The battles of Pilleth and Hyddgen are examined in detail, as is the Franco-Welsh advance on Worcester. Finally the evidence is detailed for Owain spending his last days with his daughters in Herefordshire. 256pp with photographs. £9.95 ISBN 1 873827 24 5

The Civil War in Hereford

by Ron Shoesmith. Documents from the Civil War are used to tell the history of the four sieges by Parliament of Hereford together with the accompanying strife in the county as a whole. Ironically the best prepared army led by one of the most experienced generals of the age, that of the Scots led by Alexander Leslie, Earl of Leven, was the one which failed with much loss of life. Two earlier attempts succeeded after brief skirmishes, with resultant court martials for some of the Royalist officers; the final attempt resulted in a pamphlet entitled *A new tricke to take Townes*. 176pp with maps and photographs. £8.95 ISBN 1 873827 34 2

A View from Hereford's Past

by Richard Stone and Nic Appleton-Fox, this tells of the excavation of the precincts of Hereford Cathedral in preparation for the building of the new Mappa Mundi exhibition centre. It relates several surprising finds, including over 1,100 complete skeletons and charnel of an additional 5,000 bodies. The excavation has also shed new light on the road layout and style of buildings of the Saxon city; of the diseases that prevailed amongst the medieval population and much besides. Whilst serving as the interim archaeological report, the text is written in a way that anyone interested in finding out in substantial detail what has so far emerged from the archaeological work can do so. 80pp with 44 photographs, maps and illustrations. (A4 format, bound) £9.95 ISBN 1 873827 39 3

Other books in the Monuments in the Landscape series

Vol. 1 Prehistoric Sites of Herefordshire

by George Children and George Nash, this details our knowledge of the Stone, Bronze and Iron Ages in Herefordshire, using archaeological evidence, comparisons with neighbouring areas and ethnography. The authors advance theories about how early society interacted with the landscape, especially that which they created. Herefordshire is well-known for its array of hillforts, and many of these are detailed in the site descriptions, together with earlier barrows, standing stones and chambered tombs. 144pp with some 50 photographs, plans and maps. £6.95. ISBN 1 873827 09 1

Vol. II Castles & Moated Sites of Herefordshire

by Ron Shoesmith. Herefordshire is a county of castles and moated sites, reflecting its position as a well populated agricultural county bordering disputed territory. The history of defence within the county is explained, as is that of castle building, their use and, finally, demise. There is a comprehensive gazetteer of all the sites set out parish by parish with much recent information. 256pp with some 65 photographs, plans and maps. £9.95. ISBN 1 873827 59 8

Vol. IV Prehistoric Sites of Monmouthshire

by George Children and George Nash, this is similar in format to their first volume in the series, *Prehistoric Sites of Herefordshire*. However, they have developed their theories further in the light of additional research in Monmouthshire, an area which has interesting Stone Age finds along the shores of the Severn Estuary, in addition to Bronze Age complexes, standing stones and later hillforts. 144pp with some 40 photographs, plans and maps. £7.95. ISBN 1 873827 49 0